# Before the Fall

## Preventing Pastoral Sexual Abuse

Nils C. Friberg
and
Mark R. Laaser

Published in association with the
Interfaith Sexual Trauma Institute,
Collegeville, Minnesota

*A Liturgical Press Book*

THE LITURGICAL PRESS
Collegeville, Minnesota

Cover design by Greg Becker

1    2    3    4    5    6    7    8

**Library of Congress Cataloging-in-Publication Data**

Friberg, Nils, 1935–
    Before the fall : preventing pastoral sexual abuse / Nils C.
Friberg and Mark R. Laaser.
        p.    cm.
    Includes bibliographical references.
    ISBN 0-8146-2391-3
    1. Sexual misconduct by clergy.    I. Laaser, Mark R.    II. Title.
BV4392.5.F75    1998
253'.2—dc21                                                      97-14085
                                                                      CIP

# Contents

9 8411

# Foreword

We welcome this volume that is sponsored by the Interfaith Sexual Trauma Institute. The Institute was created in May 1994 by St. John's Abbey and University in partnership with the ISTI Board to address issues within ministry of sexual abuse, exploitation, and harassment through research, education, and publication. The vision of ISTI is the building of healthy, safe, and trustworthy communities of faith.

In its statement of purpose for the institute, the ISTI Board, with membership from some fifteen Jewish and Christian traditions, strongly affirms the goodness of human sexuality and advocates respectful relationship through the appropriate use of power within communities of all religious traditions. Everyone stands to gain by examining openly together whatever we discover are the issues and by providing the means to confidently promote an informed awareness of our common failure. We must look critically at history, sexuality, human relationships, and our collective struggle to develop sexual meaning.

ISTI believes that human sexuality is sacred; misuse of power underlies all forms of sexual compromise, compromise that violates human dignity and harms individuals and communities both emotionally and spiritually. Healing and restoration are possible for survivors, offenders, and their communities through a complex and painful process. However, truth telling and justice making are integral to change and healing in individuals and institutions.

The goals of ISTI are to

- encourage understanding of sexual misconduct through interdisciplinary seminars, conferences, and seminary instruction;

- develop models of intervention, psychological and spiritual healing, restitution, and recovery of community trust in collaboration with such persons as victims, offenders, religious leaders, and those in the helping professions;
- support the systematic study of and theological reflection on healthy human sexuality and appropriate use of power;
- publish materials regarding victims and healing, offenders and rehabilitation, and spiritual communities and their transformation;
- advance research on sexual abuse, exploitation, harassment, and their prevention;
- collect and disseminate accurate information about issues of sexual misconduct;
- network with other professional organizations and agencies that deal with issues of sexual misconduct.

We welcome comments and suggestions. For information on ISTI programs and resources including the ISTI quarterly newsletter, *The ISTI Sun,* please address correspondence to:

Executive Director
Interfaith Sexual Trauma Institute
St. John's Abbey and University
Collegeville, MN 56321 U.S.A.
Phone: 320-363-3994
Fax: 320-363-3954
e-mail: isti@csbsju.edu
Internet: http://www.osb.org/isti/

# Introduction

## Need for This Book

In 1994 we surveyed 180 member institutions of the Association of Theological Schools by a mailed-out questionnaire. Of the eighty-eight responses that we received, not one disputed that clergy sexual misconduct was a very significant issue. Most noted that their schools were working closely with their denomination to keep aware and respond to the problem. *Leadership* magazine published a frequently-quoted survey in 1988 that reported on three hundred pastors who responded to their inquiry. Seventy percent reported that they felt that pastors are particularly vulnerable to sexual misconduct. When asked whether they had "ever done anything with someone (not your spouse) that you feel was sexually inappropriate," 77 percent said yes. More specifically, a later question asked: "Have you ever had sexual intercourse with someone other than your spouse since you've been in local-church ministry?" Twelve percent responded yes, and 88 percent, no.[1] These figures are supported by other surveys we have seen for therapists and clergy.[2]

One of the most active and successful lawyers in the process of seeking legal justice for victims of clergy sexual abuse has been Jeff Anderson of St. Paul, Minnesota. He has told us that he is

---

[1]"How Common Is Pastoral Indiscretion?" *Leadership* (Winter Quarter 1988) 12.

[2]Cf. *Journal of Psychology and Christianity,* ed. John F. Shackelford (Winter 1989) 8:4. We disagree strongly, however, with this editor's tendency to name clergy sexual misconduct "an affair," since it represents much more than breaking one's marital vows.

personally aware of over eight thousand legal cases involving clergy sexual abuse. He wonders out loud about what the actual number of instances of clergy sexual involvement with vulnerable people is given the fact that only a small percentage bring legal action against their perpetrator. Mr. Anderson has been outspoken in his assertion that the wider church has been involved, at least historically, in a broad cover up of the problem.

Obviously, the number of, and financial liability for, cases of clergy sexual misconduct is creating great concern among church leaders across all denominations. The growing discrediting of, and mistrust in, clergy has put furrows into many an ecclesiastical brow. In a poll published by the Twin Cities *Star Tribune* in February 1993, 2 percent of Minnesotans said they had been touched by church workers in a way that made them feel uncomfortable. Given the range of sampling error, this means that from 58,700 to 124,100 Minnesota adults have been touched by clergy in a way that may have been troubling to them.

All professionals experience a tightening up of ethical standards these days. However, it appears to us that much more needs to be done than recognize our anxiety level. A previous volume in this series under the aegis of the Interfaith Sexual Trauma Institute[3] focused on the primary and secondary victims of clergy sexual misconduct. Our intent in that volume was to alert churches to ways of helping people to find wholeness and trust again throughout the ever-widening circles of woundedness.

## Target Audience

This book is addressed to all those persons who make decisions concerning the formation of people preparing for ministry of all kinds. That is, we address ourselves mainly to church and seminary leadership of both denominational and ecumenical kinds. We also hope that other persons involved in this process of "the ministerial pipeline" can benefit from what we have to say

---

[3]Nancy Hopkins and Mark Laaser, eds., *Restoring the Soul of a Church: Healing Congregations Wounded by Clergy Sexual Misconduct* (Collegeville: The Liturgical Press, 1995). Nils C. Friberg wrote chapter five, "Wounded Congregations," 55–74.

here, whether they are candidates themselves, or local church people who want to stay informed about the causes and prevention of clergy sexual misconduct.

## Nature of This Book

This book aims at answering the question: "What can be done while people are preparing for ministry to effectively re-educate or redirect them?" This is not primarily an orientation book for seminarians nor for potential or actual victims, although such persons might find our descriptions helpful in some ways. Neither is it primarily a book on pastoral ethics, though much of what we say here has profound ethical decision-making implications both for leadership and candidates for ministry.

We are focusing chiefly in this volume on the way ecclesiastical bodies put together the plans, guidance and structures for preparation and formation of people who plan to enter the ministry. We write with an eye to a broad audience across a whole spectrum of theological positions. Thus, we do not rule out certain kinds of church bodies, though we admit that non-Christian religions may find our book less useful. We do not intend to define sexual sin nor declare a position on sexual orientation. Our objective is to help you look at the practical issues from your own theological perspective.

## How We Got Here

The two of us met in the early 1970s while both in a doctoral program, and while taking two quarters of Clinical Pastoral Education together at the University of Iowa Hospitals and Clinics. Nils came from eight years of ministry in Brazil, most of which was spent teaching in a seminary in São Paulo City. Mark was fresh out of his theological education at Princeton Theological Seminary. We thought we knew each other pretty well at the end of those four years. Along the way there were several people, including counseling supervisors, who heard major portions of Mark's concerns but who did not recognize the seriousness of his issues.

During their studies together, unknown to Nils or anyone else, Mark was struggling mightily with sexual issues, and after graduation he came to perpetrate as a pastoral counselor and be taken to court by three counseling clients. He recounts his full story in *Faithful and True*[4] and tells how he came to be involved in helping other clergy and spouses recover from sexual addiction and sexual misconduct. He is now serving as a consultant on a nationwide basis to treatment centers who deal with these issues. Mark's haunting and constant question is: "Could anyone anywhere have seen my problem and helped me prevent doing what I did?"

After obtaining his Ph.D., Nils became a professor of pastoral care in a denominational seminary in Minnesota, and over the years gradually became involved in doing work with seminarians and clergy who struggle with their sexuality or misconduct. He served as a sexual harassment officer for his institution for several years and has chaired a denominational task force that was charged with writing policy for dealing with sexual misconduct in local churches. He has been assigned to investigate and deal with several perpetrating seminary graduates, his own classmates and a couple of denominational figures. He has intervened in several churches wounded by clergy sexual misconduct and has also written on that subject. Nils' constant question is: "What could we be doing to stop this before it starts?"

## Definitions

The sensitive nature of our topic requires careful definition of a number of key terms that have often been confused:

> **Boundaries:** Rules, norms, and codes of conduct that create a safe and nurturing environment for a person emotionally, physically, sexually, and spiritually. Effective boundaries allow us to feel safe and nurtured, and to be in charge of our own areas of competence and responsibility. They may be defined and vary according to our gender, race, age, cul-

---

[4]Mark Laaser, *Faithful and True: Sexual Integrity in a Fallen World* (Grand Rapids, Mich.: Zondervan Publications, 1996). First published in 1992 under the title *The Secret Sin*.

ture, and religion. They may be either too rigid or too loose for ultimate well-being.

**Vulnerability:** A condition in which there is less than full capacity to face and resist invasion of one's own boundaries, due to some deficiency or imbalance in social, mental, spiritual, or experiential development, status, or power.

**Sexual Abuse:** Invasion of a person's sexual boundaries by a person who possesses emotional, physical, or spiritual power or influence over him or her. Sexual abuse always creates damage to the vulnerable person.

**Sexual Harassment:** The use of one's emotional, spiritual, vocational, financial or social influence/power to gain sexual access to or dominance over a person vulnerable to that influence. Harassment can also involve the creation, whether by design or not, of a hostile environment in which words, actions, artwork, gestures, humor cause such discomfort for another person that they cannot function well in that setting.

**Sexual Misconduct:** any sexual act that a person or group considers immoral or which society considers illegal. This terminology is usually employed within a professional relationship.

## Structure

We divided *Before the Fall* into two main sections, the first dealing with the nature of this problem, its etiology and assessment, and the second focusing on means of prevention applicable to the life of the candidate for ministry. Chapter one uses vignettes of seminarians to portray the ways internal and external issues might present themselves as students come into their educational experience. Chapter two describes offenders across the spectrum of types of personality. Chapter three portrays possible causes for offending. Chapter four delineates environmental conditions that heighten vulnerability to offend. Chapter five paints the picture of vulnerable counseling clients or church people.

Beginning Part Two, chapter six lays out the five major dimensions of healthy sexuality in order to have a model to constructively inform candidates for ministry. Chapter seven suggests many ways the topic of healthy sexuality can be dealt with in the seminary classroom. Chapter eight brings out the role of spiritual formation in the development of safe and healthy sexual conduct. Chapter nine discusses places in the field education process and clinical training where supervision can help students look at their sexual feelings and attitudes. Chapter ten assesses the role of community in assisting candidates for ministry to take seriously and constructively their belonging and participation in community. The Conclusion provides a summary of learning outcomes that we hope will empower educators and church leaders to thoroughly evaluate whether a candidate for ministry is indeed well prepared to serve with holistic sexual integrity and effectiveness. A Case Study terminates the book and provides discussion questions.

We have tried to avoid being too theoretical without neglecting a thoroughly informed background search on this important issue. We want this book to be a ready reference for all church and seminary leaders in their efforts to improve the ways we educate and supervise people for ministry. We would appreciate hearing from you concerning the helpful or unhelpful materials this book provides so that future editions could incorporate improved guidance on this important enterprise.

We dedicate this volume to you, the reader, and pray earnestly for divine guidance in your life as you use it. May injury to innocent people be less and less named among us in the Church of Jesus Christ. We pray for the wholeness of all our candidates for ministry in the words of the Apostle Paul: "May the God of peace himself sanctify you entirely; and may your spirit and soul and body be kept sound and blameless at the coming of our Lord Jesus Christ" (1 Thess 5:23).

# Part One
# The Problem

# Chapter One
# The Challenge

Imagine several candidates for ministry sitting in their first seminary class at any institution around the country.[1]

Randy is a first-year student at a Roman Catholic seminary. He is bright and popular with his peers. He has been successful all the way through his parochial school and college education. He is socially adept and a high achiever academically and athletically. He is glad to be pursuing what has seemed always to be the vocation he should pursue. In third grade he was voted the boy most likely to become a priest. His mother is so proud. Out of eight brothers and sisters, he is "her special son." He is the one most devoted to God. His mother has devoted special time and attention to him. Randy has not seen his father in several years, since his parents divorced several years ago, and his father lives in another state.

Gone, or so he thinks, are the memories of sexual encounters with older men during his growing up years. First, there was the man in the park who was so nice to him. Then there was his own parish priest whom he tried to tell about the older man in the park. Finally, there was one of his older brothers. He should never have to think about these things as an ordained priest. He had never cared much for girls anyway. His celibacy vow will not be a problem.

---

[1] All case examples in this book are either fictitious or used anonymously with the permission of the person. Fictitious cases are the amalgam of actual ones that we have known.

Tom enters his first year at an evangelical seminary with youthful enthusiasm and a "passion for God." He is tall, handsome, athletic, and already a powerful speaker. He has just married Jane, one of the most popular girls at a small Christian college. Together they are embarking on a career of service "wherever God may lead them."

Tom and Jane come from families that were pillars of their local church. Tom's father was an elder, and Jane's father was himself a pastor. The local church had been central to both their lives. Tom and Jane were prominent in church activities since they were small. So many things about their lives were "perfect."

Tom's mother was a "godly" woman. Jane's dad was a powerful preacher, strong, preparing and practicing his sermons with fervor. Recently he finished writing his fourth book. Jane and her mother have become especially close friends as they have watched their husband and father do such wonderful things. They have never talked about the stash of pornography that Jane once found in a corner of the garage. It was easily overlooked because "Dad is such a wonderful and effective pastor."

---

Warren's first day is at a liberal, mainline seminary. He is looking forward to a parish career that will allow him to help people understand the beauty and depth of God's creation, as well as to aid them in establishing greater justice in social institutions. He has always been artistic, loved the richness of the liturgy and music of the church.

Warren never knew his dad, who died when Warren was three. His mother did the best she could raising him. He needed to grow up fast, being the "man of the house," being depended upon by his mother "to get things done." Frequently she would take him along to church social activities. At church and at school, several older men had taken special interest in Warren, showing him kindness and attention. It frightened Warren when they began to introduce him to sexual activity, but at the same time it seemed to be part of their caring relationship with him, something he desperately needed.

---

Bill's first day is at an academically prestigious seminary. He is surprised to be here. He has finally arrived at "a bastion of academic excellence." He feels smarter just being there. His grades were never perfect, but evidently good enough to get him in. His social and personal life are deeply affected by his preoccupation with viewing videos. He has had a daily masturbation habit. He hopes that getting married will help him stop all of this.

Bill's family is an average middle-class one. Bill's father is a blue-collar worker, and while he drinks a lot, he has never caused a major problem. Bill's mother loves food and is extremely overweight. While she loves to cook, clean, and maintain the house, she has never had an emotional or spiritual conversation with Bill. Bill's dad has depended upon him to be his "special friend." While there has been much sexual humor in the house, sex has never been discussed.

Bill has always been popular and has dated lots of women. He always had long and intense relationships with them. He will finally marry one of these half way through his seminary career. Bill, since childhood, has struggled with sexual fantasies and desires. He has used lots of pornographic magazines and videos.

Mary, Bill's wife, has a father who is a very successful businessman. In many respects Mary's family is ideal. In her own mind, not quite as popular as her older sister, she has nevertheless compensated by excelling academically and socially. Mary's family has also never talked about sex except for Mary's mother's warnings about its dangers. The family has never gone to church, but Mary's own spiritual quest leads her to look forward to being a pastor's wife.

---

Sandra is proud to be one of the first female candidates from her seminary. She is looking forward to the life of a pastor. She is hoping, for the most part unconsciously, that ordination will be a transforming moment, erasing much of the pain of her past. She is in seminary searching for a role and power that have traditionally only belonged to men. Her seminary is proud to admit a person of such high academic achievement.

Sandra is an incest victim by her father, uncle, and brother. Her mother slapped her when she tried to talk about what was happening. The only escape she could discover from her incestuous and physically abusive family was at church. She has excelled academically her entire high school and college career. At her Christian college she became sexually involved with one of her professors. Her dating relationships frightened her because, for reasons that mystify her, she selects men who are verbally and emotionally abusive. Sandra also becomes sexually involved with one of her field education supervisors. He is older, experienced, a real father type.

———

All of these students have obviously been accepted at seminary due to a variety of factors. There are no immediately *observable* problems of their conduct in their past. Each of their institutions has required an MMPI II (Minnesota Multiphasic Personality Inventory II) at admission, which has failed to reveal any marked pathology. All of their grades are adequate. They have been glowingly recommended by pastors, church leaders, and teachers. They are social and outgoing. All have been athletes. They have been able to articulate an appropriate faith stance and energetically claim a call to ministry. They certainly do not appear to be trying to escape any problems.

## Outcomes

In his tenth year of parish ministry, Randy is arrested by the police. He has been reported to them by several outraged fathers who have discovered that Randy was sexual with their sons. The bishop is currently investigating the charges and has removed Randy from active ministry.

After twenty years in the ministry, Tom's elder board calls him into a specially arranged session. Several women of the church have come forward to allege sexual relationships with him. Jane is included in this meeting, and both Tom and Jane are devastated by these revelations. The elders instruct him to pack his bags and look for another church immediately. He will be allowed to preach on Sunday, but not allowed to mention anything about the cause of his departure.

As Warren enters his first year of ministry in his third parish, he is arrested for soliciting male prostitutes. To his superiors, he makes the claim this is his first offense, but in his heart he knows it is not. Warren's wife, at one level, is surprised by this news, but at another level, it seems to make sense in terms of the way their relationship has gone. Warren's denomination is currently debating the possibility of homosexual ordinations. Everyone is confused by this situation. There is no adequate response really possible at this time.

Bill's masturbation habit developed into a pattern of seeking prostitutes when he was in graduate school obtaining a degree in pastoral counseling. In his tenth year of counseling practice he is intervened on by his professional colleagues for having sex with one of his clients. The woman who came forward is the tenth victim in a succession of exploitative relationships Bill has had with clients. Bill and Mary now are without income and face the prospect of years of therapy and the probability of numerous lawsuits. The lawyers for Bill's denomination are advising them to deal quickly with the situation, but they have very little contact with him in the process.

In her seminary and clinical training process, Sandra has experienced several brief affairs with professors and supervisors. She also experienced numerous events of sexual harassment by fellow students. In her first parish Sandra discovers that she continues to date abusive men. She is depressed at her ability to form meaningful relationships. Five years into ministry she has a brief affair with one of the members of her congregation. In her shame she reports this to her denominational superior. He advises her to discontinue the affair, get some therapy, and not to mention it again.

———

Why are we surprised by these outcomes with Randy, Tom, Warren, Bill, and Sandra? By all indications of their admissions data, including psychometric testing, these were apparently normal students. That is why we are surprised. They were successful academically and socially. Sadly, these cases are all too reflective of situations that have shocked and grieved most religious bodies and denominations. Given this, many are asking whether theological institutions can actually screen out potential sexual problems including offenses. The quick answer to that is a probable "no." If we are forced to depend only upon psychological testing instruments, admission interviews and references, we will not be successful screening out offenders.

We mailed out surveys to 210 seminaries. About eighty-five of them responded. We will refer to the information throughout this book. The overwhelming consensus of seminary administration and faculty response was that potential offenders could not be detected through traditional psychometric means. We suggest that there are two reasons for this. First is that traditional psychometric testing has not been able to adequately assess risk factors. Second, sexual misconduct may be based on factors external to the offender as well as on internal causes.

There may be exceptions to this. There will be applicants with gross levels of pathology. For example, MMPIs with high scores on psychopathic deviate and mania scales (scales 4 and 9), and others who have a mixture of schizophrenic thinking (scale 8), may be particularly vulnerable to acting out, pushing by people's boundaries in sexual and other ways. This level of pathology is not often seen in candidates for ministry. The academic and social process that they have gone through to get to the position of being a candidate for ministry will have already screened out the more serious cases.

On the other hand, in the above described cases, we could have seen that these students came from backgrounds that made them vulnerable to the possibility of sexual misconduct. In each one there were varying degrees of sexual, physical, emotional, and spiritual abuse. In all of their families boundaries were confused, there were incidents of various addictions. This vulnerability can be described as including the following factors:

- these students are arrested at various stages of psychosexual development;
- they have poor skills for intimacy, resulting in unsatisfactory relationships and no real friendships;
- they are able to lead congregations but not participate in community themselves;
- they have been externally focused on their role, status, power, and connections with other people for a sense of their worth;
- they are not good at nurturing themselves physically, emotionally, or spiritually;
- these students are extremely vulnerable to the isolation and stress of their role and the needs of their parishioners;
- they can lead the formal practice of religion but are not able to experience an internally healthy spiritual relationship with God.

This list of characteristics of these five people describes a general condition of risk. In itself, this list does not necessarily predict sexual misconduct. The factors we have described could lead to a variety of dysfunctions other than sexual misconduct. In order that there be sexual misconduct, other factors must be in place. If sexual misconduct includes sexual offense against vulnerable adults or children, there must be three risk factors: the state of the offender, the vulnerability of the victim, and stressful environmental conditions. The offending moment will always involve a complex interaction of all of these factors. *Figure 1* below illustrates this interaction.

The students that we described illustrate the vulnerability of the offender. As we will discuss in chapter two, the depth of this vulnerability will vary on a continuum between health and pathology. In other words, some people will be more vulnerable than others. Some offenders will be more active. Some will be more passive.

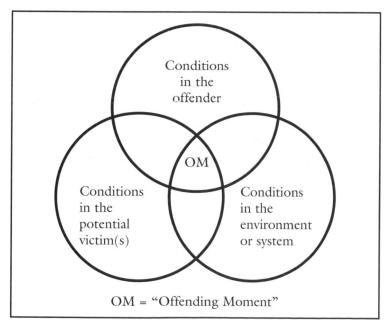

*Figure 1:* Model of "The Offending Moment"

Joyce Ridick, S.S.C., in her treatment of counseling seminarians, recommends that seminaries alert potential students about a list of issues that might cause them problems in ministry, and asks students to get psychological counseling before applying. Her list is long and comprehensive, but a few examples give us the tenor of her recommendation:[2]

- unresolved addiction to alcohol, drugs, sex;
- unresolved abuse as a child, which interferes with one's present functioning;
- pathologies related to family dysfunctions;
- serious developmental deficits.

This list is a helpful start. The factors we believe important to look for are:

- family background
- addiction history
- psychosexual development
- history of abuse
- cognitive beliefs and values
- psychological and spiritual maturity
- neurochemistry

What is possible to predict are the environmental factors which our students will encounter. These factors will include:

- the systems of their church
- the systems of their local communities
- culturally learned attitudes, beliefs, and patterns
- marital stress
- family stress
- economic stress
- vocational stress

If any kind of offending takes place, it will also depend upon the vulnerabilities of the people the offender works with. This vulnerability will mirror the risk factors of the offender. These factors include:

---

[2]Joyce Ridick, *Psychology, Counseling and The Seminarian,* ed. Robert J. Wister (Washington, D.C.: National Catholic Educational Association, 1994) 67–92.

- history of abuse
- family background
- psychosexual development
- cognitive beliefs and values
- psychological and spiritual maturity
- neurochemistry

Figure 1 suggests that an offending moment will occur at the intersection and interaction of these factors. There will be times when one set of factors is more important than the others. For example, the pathology of an offender may be so severe that they will act out despite the absence of relative stresses in the other areas. The case of James Porter illustrates how a Catholic priest can offend repeatedly over time with a great variety of environmental factors and victim vulnerabilities.

There are other times when the environmental factors will be so stressful as to overwhelm an otherwise relatively healthy individual. This will be true particularly if this individual has not been trained concerning the dynamics of congregational life and the potential dangers of misconduct.

We must also recognize that the vulnerabilities of the victim may be so severe that they will aggressively pursue acts of misconduct. We would *never* say that a victim is responsible for misconduct. But we must recognize that their pathology may be the overriding factor in a particular situation of misconduct. This is particularly so when the offender has not been trained to understand this level of vulnerability. This will involve ignorance of or inexperience in dealing with the problematic dynamics of transference and countertransference. We know of many cases, for example, in which a relatively naïve and untrained pastor has been overwhelmed by a person with borderline personality disturbance. One of the borderline features was a need to be involved, even sexually, with a person in power. This again raises the issue of the churches' responsibility to do an adequate job of training candidates for ministry.

Our model also suggests that there will be moments of misconduct that occur that do not involve a victim. The area in which the environmental factors and vulnerability of the pastor intersect illustrates that there may be acts involving such things as pornography, compulsive masturbation, prostitution, affairs with non-vulnerable adults, exhibitionism, to name only the most common forms. These are sexual acts that most religious traditions would consider sinful. If the candidate for ministry is cooperative, and if we have a good understanding of the factors that often contribute to potential capability of inappropriate crossing of sexual boundaries or misuse of one's power, we may be more successful than we have been in the past detecting potential for misconduct.

It would be preferable for counseling to be successfully completed before application to seminary. Admissions offices will need to balance the need to recruit students with the necessary cautions laid down by Ridick and others. It appears that with churches calling for graduates who are "safe" and the rising concerns of students around invasion of their privacy, seminaries have some uncomfortable tensions to face.

Admissions officers face several limitations concerning what they can ask applicants. It does not seem probable, however, that we would be limited in describing for applicants the necessary foundations for personal health and successful life in ministry and ask them to work on those foundations with thoroughness before entering seminary. It would then be important to keep raising before current seminary students the kinds of issues they need to be continuing to be alert for, and thus lay the onus for response upon the students themselves. Legitimate doubts about the capacity of students to know themselves this well might be raised here. Some kind of structure for ongoing awareness needs to be in place at the seminary, and careful observation of each student's interpersonal and social performance throughout class work and field education would be appropriate. We will be describing this in Part Two of this book.

In this book we are not positing a static, definable "x," direct cause and effect factors that will always lead to sexual misconduct. We are attempting to describe a set of conditions embedded in a person's inner life, which under certain conditions, and given an attractive opportunity, may emerge in a decision to "cross the line."

We can describe the general conditions of vulnerability; we cannot predict with certainty how the individual will use or succumb to the conditions. We hypothesize that the more conditions from all three of the above circles are present and actively exerting their influence on the situation, the greater the possibility of sexual misconduct. We will note as we proceed that it is very difficult to describe any one of these circles without drawing upon information from the other two. There is frequent overlap and interchange between them. The circles do, however, help us to identify the major arenas to be treated for effective outcomes in prevention.

The reality is that all that we can do is discover vulnerability to sexual misconduct. The choices made by the potential perpetrator are subject to a variety of factors, as our model suggests. Our model of the offending moment, therefore, indicates that three areas of concern will be important for prevention at the formation level. First, we must try as best we can to assess over the time the psychological and spiritual maturity of the candidate for ministry. Where possible or necessary, we should seek to make therapeutic and spiritually directive intervention. Our belief is that the ideal purpose of screening is not to exclude candidates from ministry but to identify areas that need healing before active ministry can proceed.

Second, we need to educate seminarians about the tremendous power of their role and its effect on other people. Further, certain people will be more vulnerable to that power than others, and the seminarian needs to be able to recognize that danger. Seminarians should be made aware of their own motivations for entering ministry and how they might be overly attracted to the use of power in ministry. Recent prevention strategies such as Marie Fortune's work, have been very helpful in educating us about necessary boundaries in the pastoral relationship.[3]

Third, our model suggests that environmental factors will be critical. Seminarians, therefore, must be well educated and instructed on the disciplines of self-care. In Part Two we will present a model of healthy sexuality that will describe the nature of this discipline.

---

[3]Marie Fortune, *Clergy Misconduct: Sexual Abuse in the Ministerial Relationship,* workshop manual (Seattle: Center for the Prevention of Sexual and Domestic Violence, 1992) 21.

Any of these areas emphasized in isolation are possibly doomed to failure. For example, if we educate only about boundaries, yet psychopathology exists in the seminarian that allow him/her to cross boundaries, no amount of education will be preventive in the true sense. Conversely, the healthiest seminarian, psychologically and spiritually, left unaware of dangerous risks in the parish setting, might fall prey to those risks. Finally, a mature and well-educated seminarian, unprotected from the stresses of the ministry, can also succumb to its dangers or pitfalls.

In Part Two we will present our view of how we must deal with the interaction of these factors. We will do so in the context of a model of healthy sexuality that describes how an individual might heal from personal vulnerabilities and avoid the stresses of environment and the vulnerabilities of others. The next chapters describe in detail the exact nature of each of the three spheres of our model of sexual misconduct.

# Chapter Two

# Clergy and Sexual Misconduct—Characteristics

We will devote two chapters to understanding clergy who sexually act out and/or offend. Much of this chapter has been influenced by several hundred cases that we have personally known. Very little hard research data or sound clinical theorizing exists about sexual misconduct specific to clergy.[1] We divide this chapter into two sections: theories about sexual misconduct and clergy, and theories about sexual offending and clergy.

## Sexual Offending and Clergy

There has been some effort to describe types of sexually offending therapists. This is useful in itself for understanding offending clergy since much of the work that clergy do is in the context of counseling and because of similarities in the power of both therapist and clergy roles. Some of this work can be extrapolated to clergy. Some original work exists about clergy specifically, and we will summarize these studies.

---

[1]Mark Laaser has addressed this issue in two places. The entire issue of *Pastoral Psychology* (March 1991) 39:4, is devoted to this topic. See specifically his article, "Sexual Addiction and Clergy," 213–35. See also chapter five of his *Faithful and True: Sexual Integrity in a Fallen World* (Grand Rapids, Mich.: Zondervan Publications, 1996).

Theories of therapist sexual offending usually describe those who demonstrate severe pathology on one end of the spectrum to those with less severe but more frequently seen conditions on the other. Two of the major voices in this field have been Gary Schoener and John Gonsiorek at the Walk-In Counseling Center in Minneapolis. With the broad experience of diagnosing hundreds of therapist and clergy offenders, they described nine categories of sexual offenders:

1. The naïve offender is ignorant of professional sexual ethics and does not understand and is unprepared to deal with the power differentials involved in care-giving settings.
2. The normal or mildly neurotic professional may develop a gradual romantic relationship with a vulnerable person during a stressful time in his/her own life.
3. The severely neurotic or socially isolated professional will display longer term personality traits such as depression, inadequacy, low self-esteem, and social isolation. This person may demonstrate a repetitive pattern of offending. He/she will seek to be self-punitive rather than changing the problematic behavior and has poor boundaries about caretaking of vulnerable others.
4. Professionals with impulsive character disorders include a wide variety of inappropriate behavior, including even criminal acts, dramatic behavioral disinhibition, but not by cunning or planning.
5. Sociopathic or narcissistic personalities will be more deliberate, cunning, and manipulative. They set out to offend more intentionally than category 4.
6. Psychotics demonstrate impaired reality testing and have delusional thinking.
7. "Classic" sex offenders have a chronic and repetitive manner of offending, including pedophiles or other types of sex offenders. They may be impulsive and narcissistic.
8. The medically disabled experience mood disorder problems, especially bi-polar disease (manic-depression), in which there is a decided lack of moral judgment.
9. Masochistic, self-defeating individuals experience internal conflicts about setting boundaries and limits. They

increasingly give in to demanding and needy or vulnerable people.[2]

These categories are academically helpful in understanding features of sexual offenders. In our own experience of talking with offenders, however, we have found that no one fits neatly and only into one of these categories. Usually they have a composite of features.

We lack incidence studies concerning frequency of the categories. In candidates for ministry or ministerial populations the last four categories (6–9) are more uncommon. Candidates possessing these traits would not usually be able to pass the admissions processing and reference screens. Incidence of one of these types, however, creates huge media attention and leads us to believe that all clergy are like this.

Glen Gabbard, a psychiatrist at Menninger Clinic, Topeka, describes four major types of offending professionals: (1) psychotic disorders; (2) predatory psychopathy and paraphilias; (3) love-sickness; (4) masochistic surrender. The two most relevant for clergy are numbers 2 and 3. Under number 3, Gabbard lists a variety of subcategories, as follows: unconscious reenactment of incestuous longings; a wish for maternal nurturance misperceived as sexual; interlocking enactments of rescue fantasies; viewing clients as an idealized version of the self; confusion of their own needs with the client's needs; fantasies that love in and of itself is curative; repression or disavowal of rage at the client's persistent thwarting of therapeutic efforts; anger at the organization one works for or at one's counseling supervisor; manic defense against mourning and grief when terminating counseling; the exception fantasy (I can get away with this one! Or, the rules don't apply to me!); insecurity about one's own masculine identity; the client seen as a transformational object; settling down by a female therapist of the "rowdy" male client; conflicts around sexual orientation.[3]

---

[2]John C. Gonsiorek, "Assessment for Rehabilitation of Exploitative Health Care Professionals and Clergy," *Breach of Trust: Sexual Exploitation by Health Care Professionals and Clergy*, ed. Gonsiorek (Thousand Oaks, Calif.: Sage Publications, 1995) 145–62.

[3]Glen O. Gabbard, "Psychotherapists Who Transgress Sexual Boundaries with Patients," ibid., 135–44.

Marie Fortune has written and trained extensively in the field of clergy sexual abuse. Her primary attention is given to victims and exposing dangers to them. In looking specifically at clergy who abuse, she agrees with the concept of a spectrum of clergy offenders. She sees it on a continuum from "wanderers" to "sexual predators." Wanderers are fairly naïve and cross boundaries, perhaps ignorant of the damage they have done. Predators are sociopathic and lack conscience.

She also lists traits of all sexual abusers in ministry that appear somewhere on the continuum: controlling, dominating, limited self-awareness, limited or no awareness of boundary issues, no sense of damage caused by their own behavior, poor judgment, limited impulse control, limited understanding of consequences of their actions, often charismatic, sensitive, talented, inspirational and effective in ministry, limited or no awareness of their own power, lack of recognition of their own sexual feelings, confusion of sex and affection.[4] Persons with such characteristics may create all kinds of problems with congregations before any sexual misconduct occurs.

Dr. Richard Irons has been involved in the assessment of impaired professionals including medical doctors, psychologists and clergy. Building on the work of Schoener and Gonsiorek, Irons has formulated an archetypal categorization of sexual offenders. As applied to clergy, he describes the following categories:

1. *The Naïve Prince.* This clergyperson is usually psychologically healthy but is inadequately trained to perceive appropriate ethical standards and boundaries. He/she may be young in ministry and experiences the power of ministerial status, feeling invulnerable. Given the right circumstances and stress level, this person can become romantically and sexually involved before the error is recognized.

2. *The Wounded Warrior.* The church becomes the professional identity of this type. They usually become im-

---

[4]Marie Fortune, *Clergy Misconduct: Sexual Abuse in the Ministerial Relationship,* workshop manual (Seattle: Center for the Prevention of Sexual and Domestic Violence, 1992) 21.

mersed in a demanding ministry. They neglect self-care. Serving others is their main source of self-worth. Shame is a central issue for these people, so validation must come from the outside. Sexual validation may be an antidote to shame. Repressed wounds from the past merge and fuel current conflicts. The warrior becomes increasingly isolated, wounded by his/her secret life. Addictive disease including sexual addiction may be present.

3. *The Self-Serving Martyr.* Clergy in this category usually are in their middle or late career. They have devoted their life to service to the church and sacrificed time for their own personal growth and family. They usually meet their personal needs through their work. Despite their need to be "the ultimate caregiver," this type comes to resent the demands of the congregation. They feel unappreciated and abandoned. Anger and resentment lead them to feelings of self-justifying entitlement, which leads them across sexual boundaries into misconduct. Long-suffering martyrs may become highly narcissistic and develop beliefs that they have a special ministry that God has created for them and that no one else fully understands them. This type experiences significant inner conflicts and anxiety, with a variety of addictions possible, including sexual addiction. Characterological pathology such as obsessive-compulsive, narcissistic, dependent, or hysterical types are possible.

4. *The False Lover.* This type lives a life of intensity and high drama. They love living life on the edge, taking risks, including the thrill of seducing another in an act of passion and conquest. They are fixated adolescents. They may be charming, creative and energetic, often creating the impression that they are the best minister who has ever served this congregation. Religiosity is often used as a cover to convince others of a deep spirituality. Sexual misconduct takes place both in and out of the congregation. False lovers may maintain a series of lovers with multiple, concurrent partners. They may live a life full

of divorces, job changes, and other social, legal, and vocational vacillation. Characterological pathology is similar to the self-serving martyr.

5. *The Dark King.* This clergyman is best described as
charming and charismatic, exploiting his or her power
for personal gain. He or she is grandiose and needs to
control and dominate. They can usually find a vulnerable adult to meet their sexual needs. The charisma of
this type usually creates devoted followers who will remain fiercely loyal even when sexual misconduct is exposed. Dark Kings will go to great lengths to defend
themselves and are usually therapeutically and legally
adept enough to do this in a convincing fashion. While
this type is rare, it is usually the one we find in media
portrayals. It also represents a type of leader from which
a congregation has great difficulty recovering.

6. *The Wild Card.* These people suffer from major mental
disorders. If left untreated by professionals, this person
may seek to manage their illness with sexual activity.
Theirs is not part of a well-defined pattern or ritual.
They may appear religious, and their spirituality may in
fact be genuine.[5]

Carolyn Bates and Annette M. Brodski present an analysis of
the issues involved in therapists' sexual misconduct. They also
present a spectrum of those who offend. At one end are those
therapists who are "in love." These therapists are younger and
more inexperienced. They are usually only sexually involved with
one patient. They have been inadequately trained and fail to see
the true nature of the power imbalance in the relationship. Next
are therapists with a personality disorder. Brodski and Bates consider the offender's personality as most commonly an "antisocial
disorder." These offenders may have multiple partners. They

---

[5]Richard Irons and Katherine Roberts, "The Unhealed Wounder," *Restoring
the Soul of the Church: Healing Congregations Wounded by Clergy Sexual Misconduct,* ed. Mark Laaser and Nancy Hopkins (Collegeville: The Liturgical Press,
1995) 33–51.

present themselves as caring professionals and elicit the trust of their patients. These are the most dangerous therapists. Finally, at the other end of the spectrum, Brodski and Bates admit that there are falsely accused professionals, a rare but real occurrence. They estimate that these accusations may result from perceptual problems between the therapist and client. For example, the patient may interpret incorrectly that the therapist is encouraging feelings of sexual arousal.[6]

Assessment theories have been primarily presented around an understanding of male offenders, since the large majority of offenders are male. Irons and Roberts, e.g., say that in their sample of two hundred professionals, five were women. Cultural bias, however, may affect how many female therapists are reported. Hankins et al contend that male victims are much less prone to portray offenses by female therapists as negative.[7]

One offending female pastor with whom we talked told us the story that when she reported herself to her bishop, he told her to be quiet about it. He said that men are always in control of the sexual situation.

Ann Bartram, a female therapist and pastor, is quite candid that women pastors can have quite strong sexual feelings toward parishioners and counseling clients. For example, she describes that the males in her experience that women are prone to act out with are especially those who are needy, vulnerable, and lonely.[8]

Historically and culturally, women therapists are less frequently in superior positions of power over males, so the incidence of sexual misconduct reflects that. However, there is probably good reason to say that in our culture women are sexually less aggressive.

Very little research has been done that is specific to clergy sex offenders. One such study was conducted by Richard Irons and Mark Laaser with a group of twenty-five clergy, all of whom had

[6]Carolyn M. Bates and Annette M. Brodsky, *Sex in the Therapy Hour: A Case of Professional Incest* (New York: Guilford Press, 1989) 135–6.

[7]Gary C. Hankins and others, "Patient-Therapist Sexual Involvement: A Review of Clinical and Research Data," *Bulletin of the American Academy of Psychiatry and Law* (1994) 22:1, 109–26.

[8]Ann Bartram, "A Response to Pastor-Client Sexual Relations," *Pastoral Care and Liberation Praxis*, ed. Perry LeFevre and W. Widdick Schroeder (Chicago: Exploration Press, 1986) 37–50.

been reported for various levels of sexual misconduct. Twenty-one of the participants had at least one identified victim, but the average number of victims was two. The researchers suspected that the participants were not entirely honest about the number of victims.[9] All of the offenders were classified by the DMS-IIIR categories. Six of these pastors were felt to meet the criteria for a "personality disorder." Three were classified as "narcissistic." The other three were diagnosed as having "a personality disorder not-otherwise-specified (NOS)." Fifteen demonstrated characteristics strong enough to be considered by DMS-IIIR as "personality traits," that is, patterns of personality problems not strong enough to be considered a full-blown disorder.

Eleven of these pastors were found to have narcissistic personality problems of some degree. Nine of them were considered to have dependent personally traits. Eight of them were diagnosed as obsessive-compulsive, an anxiety disorder. These findings suggest that while narcissism may be a primary issue, we must also look for coexisting anxiety disorders and dependent personalities. This creates a combination of a need for validation and affirmation on the one hand, but an exterior appearance of not needing anyone, even to the extent of being blatantly unconcerned about what others think of them. Thoburn and Balswick describe this in terms of pastors looking constantly for signs that they are not a failure, but a success. These men look for affirmation from women out of their own low self-esteem and neediness.[10]

Irons and Laaser also found that nine of the participants had problems with alcoholism or alcohol abuse. Three suffered from major depression, six from a less severe form of depression, and nine from mixed emotional features including depression and anxiety. Fifteen of them were diagnosed as having a sexual disorder of some type, most commonly sexual compulsivity/addiction.

This study bears witness to the validity of the spectrum. There were several very serious level offenders, with profound disease;

[9]Richard Irons and Mark Laaser, "The Abduction of Fidelity: Sexual Exploitation by Clergy—Experience with Inpatient Assessment," *Sexual Addiction and Compulsivity* (1994) 1:2, 119–29.

[10]John W. Thoburn and Jack O. Balswick, "An Evaluation of Infidelity Among Male Protestant Clergy," *Pastoral Psychology* (1994) 42:4, 285–94.

there were several cases of men with less severe disease that seemed to have made some honest misjudgments. Some of the participants suffered from addictive/compulsive behavior disorders, but not all. These men were primarily middle-aged. The median age of the sample was forty-nine. They had functioned in ministry for at least twenty-five years. They were able to achieve some success in ministry but had been hiding their problems all along. None of the pastors was diagnosed with sociopathic disorder. Only one presented with antisocial traits. It seems likely that the most common offender is going to be a person who does not present with extreme forms of mental problems.

Psychometrically, we might uncover a person who does demonstrate severe pathology; for example, an MMPI II with spikes on the 4 and 9 scales, which means that the person is rebelling against authority and has the energy to carry out harmful behaviors. However, the above sample in the Irons-Laaser study suggests that by these psychometric criteria, twenty-four of the twenty-five offenders would not have been detected.

It becomes clear that diagnostically it is fairly rare to see a person at the severe end of the spectrum (*The Dark King*, or sociopathic disorder person). It is far more common to see offenders who are naïve, young, uneducated, or inexperienced. It is also far more common to find offenders in the mid-range of the spectrum with a constellation of personality and emotional factors.

In the Irons-Laaser study, for example, one pastor presented with a diagnosis of narcissistic and dependent personality traits. This person was also addicted to alcohol and sexual activity of a variety of forms. We cannot rely simply on finding severe mental pathology. We must look at vulnerability, e.g., lack of education, naïveté, family of origin dysfunction, or emotional neediness based on early childhood trauma. The presence of addictive behaviors also may indicate the possibility of offending. Whoever is screening seminarians should be familiar with addictive disease of all kinds.

Participants in the Irons-Laaser study had not only victimized vulnerable people, some had also been involved in a variety of sexual activities. This included compulsive use of pornography, fantasies, masturbation, and prostitution. There were also some paraphilic behaviors present such as exhibitionism and voyeurism.

What this suggests is that in some cases of clergy sexual offending, a diagnosis of sexual addiction may be helpful.[11]

## Sexual Misconduct and Clergy

Sexual misconduct can include any form of sexual behavior outside culturally or theologically held norms, ethics, or morality. One early study by the editors of *Leadership* magazine surveyed, through a mailed out questionnaire, a large number of its pastoral readership. Twenty-three percent of the respondents reported having committed some form of sexual misconduct.[12] Jeff Seat, Ph.D., surveyed a group of Southern Baptist pastors.[13] He received responses from 277 pastors. 14.1 percent of the respondents admitted to inappropriate sexual activity as they defined inappropriate. 10.1 percent of the entire sample disclosed that they had been sexual either with a current or former member of their churches. We can conclude that sexual misconduct is prevalent among clergy, and that the sanctity of the role does not prevent sexual problems.

Undoubtedly, there are pastors who commit various acts of sexual misconduct or abuse for whom the commission is a one time or infrequent occurrence. Many of them learn from the experience, are repentant, make confession and amends, and move on with their lives. Some of the acts of misconduct may be due to environmental circumstances (which we will discuss in chapter five) or their own situational and transient difficulties. There are others, however, who commit acts of sexual misconduct in an ongoing pattern. With them we must consider if they suffer from sexual addiction.

Sexual addiction may be defined as a pathological relationship to any form of sexual activity.[14] The pathology is that for a sex

---

[11]Sexual addiction has not been recognized as a diagnosis by the DSM-IV. We use it, however, as it has come to be accepted by many clinicians in the field.

[12]T. Muck, "How Common Is Pastoral Indiscretion?" *Leadership* 9:1 (1988) 12.

[13]Jeff T. Seat and others, "The Prevalence and Contributing Factors of Sexual Misconduct among Southern Baptist Pastors in Six Southern States," *Journal of Pastoral Care* (Winter 1993) 363–72.

[14]Patrick Carnes, *Out of the Shadows: Understanding Sexual Addiction* (Minneapolis: CompCare Publications, 1983).

addict sexual activity has become totally unmanageable. Whatever they are doing, though they intend to stop, they cannot. The amount of sexual activity becomes progressively worse and usually leads to some form of negative consequences. Sexual addiction is obviously based on feelings of genuine sexual lust; however, like many addictions the genuinely pleasurable feelings of sex can be used as an escape from painful emotions.

Carnes says that sex addicts are extremely shame-based individuals who do not believe that anyone really knows or likes them or that anyone could possibly meet their needs. Sex becomes their most important need. Sexual activity, whether a fantasy or encounter, comes to symbolize love and nurture. Carnes has also said that although sex addicts are very shameful, they are also very dependent, yet they may act as if they are very powerful.[15]

Since sexual addiction is a progressive disease, diagnosing it early in the life of a candidate for ministry would be extremely important. It is common for sexually addicted pastors who go on to offend, to tell us that in seminary their sexual acting out was in beginning stages. They had not yet offended against others. If it were possible to detect the presence of sexual addiction at an early level and therapy could be provided, later incidence of more serious sexual activity including clergy sexual abuse might be prevented. Given the shame-based nature of sexual addiction, it might be difficult to get some seminarians to admit to the problem. If we can raise consciousness about sexual addiction and its consequences, and if we let them know that help is available, they may eventually seek it. We will have more to say about letting them know about sexual addiction in a later chapter.

In this book we are mainly concentrating on those ministers who sexually offend. However, there are a far greater number who suffer with compulsive forms of sexual acting out that do not involve victims. Most commonly there are those who struggle with fantasy, masturbation, pornography, and/or prostitution. We know one pastor, for example, who is currently in jail because his prostitution habit was so excessive that he began to rob banks to pay for it. Frequent is the story of the pastor who has a stash

[15]Patrick Carnes, *Don't Call It Love: Recovery from Sexual Addiction* (New York: Bantam Books, 1991).

of pornography. There are those who have problems with masturbation, acting out several times a day, or occasional struggles with excess. We know of one pastor who masturbated twice a day for so many years that he finally needed surgery to correct the damage he had inflicted on himself.

Others may become involved in paraphilic behaviors, many of which can become quite perverse and extreme. These might include exhibitionism, voyeurism, fratteurism, bestiality, obscene phone calls, and sado-masochistic behaviors. We know of one pastor, for example, who would undress in his office and would call female parishioners about church business and masturbate to the sound of their voices. Another pastor would ride crowded city buses so that he could press up against and touch women. Another went to the health club wearing clothes in the gymnasium that would expose himself during certain forms of exercise.

Another common case that we have seen is of the pastor who is married but who struggles with acting out homosexually. One particular man that Mark Laaser worked with used his free time to "cruise" gay connecting points at public bathrooms, such as highway rest stops. He would act out like this anonymously several times per week. Obviously there are those in this category who go on to offend with same sex members of their congregations.

Sex addicts in general suffer from chronic depression. Their tolerance to pain is usually so well developed they may not be aware or fully accept that they are depressed. Due to the nature of the pastoral role, it is easy to deny one's need for help, i.e., pastors are not supposed to have problems. Many sex addicts contemplate suicide. Pastors, however, may be less prone to suicidal ideation. Some may use fear of eternal consequences to help avoid preoccupation with suicide.

The pastoral role is a potential problem for a pastor who is sexually addicted. It is relatively isolated, allows for lots of unsupervised time, and places pastors on such pedestals that they become afraid to ask for help. The vocational consequences that they would suffer also may prevent many of them from self-disclosing.

We have found that many sexually addicted pastors will often disguise their anger and their loneliness in their preaching. One priest that we knew told ostensibly humorous stories about his family that was a thinly disguised attack on them. The stories were really about his loneliness and his anger about being lonely. This kind of preaching allows for church members to give pastors rather superficial support after church service without really knowing what specifically their pastors are talking about.

Many pastors may use sexual humor in their conversations and even in their preaching. Sexual humor is a well known way that many sex addicts cover their feelings of sexual tension.

Sex addicts may by rigid and black and white in their thinking. Sexually addicted pastors may be rather theologically rigid. We think of the example of Jimmy Swaggert. His rigidity took the form in his preaching of blaming culture for battles that he was fighting inside of himself. Often he would rail against the "pimps, prostitutes, and pornographers" that plague our culture. His sociological observations may be correct, but the intensity and the tears with which he preached them seem to reveal a form of reaction formation, being angry at others for tensions that are present inside oneself.

A pastor who commits sexual sin must find ways to self-justify. Various denials and delusions can be used. One of the most common that we have seen is the "Potiphar's wife syndrome," or the "Delilah Defense." These biblical stories (Gen 39:7-20; Judg 4:16-20) are about women who sexually chased men and got them into trouble. Sexually addicted pastors may blame others for chasing them and "forcing" them to abandon their values. Another common delusion we call the "Caring Delusion." Sexually addicted pastors may feel that since their pastor activity is caring, nothing that they really do hurts anybody. Sex addicts believe that sex is equal to love, so even sex with another person is really about love. So many pastors that we have talked to who have sexually abused members of their congregations have a hard time believing that the activity really harmed others. There are also cases of pastors who passionately preach concerning God's forgiving nature who are really not facing their own misconduct.

One of the most fascinating features that we have seen with pastors who have committed sexual misconduct is the reason that they entered ministry in the first place. There are many of them who hoped that by entering ministry, their sexual misconduct would stop. Mark Laaser has called this "Ordination as a shame-reduction strategy." Some priests, for example, may hope that the vow of celibacy will help them not be sexual at all. When they find out that this does not work, it leads them to feel doubly shamed. They were bad before; now they are really bad. There are others who hope that the act of ordination will completely transform them. One woman that we talked to, who was involved in sadomasochism and had been sexual with numerous men in her congregation, reported to us that she had hope that her ordination would be a matter of "ontological transformation." She really wanted to be different. When she continued to act out, she began to wonder if she had been ordained in the wrong denomination. She despaired, "My ordination didn't take."

There are a great number of clergy, in our experience, who enter ministry because of their families' or someone else's expectation. Even from early ages they have been singled out to be religious and to enter religious service. One priest we know refers to his experience as being "ordained by my mother and not by God." This phenomenon leads eventually to an anger about one's role. This anger can often lead a sexually addicted pastor to (even unconsciously) desire to sabotage a role they do not really want.

Many clergy have been trained to be caregivers from an early age. They may have been the heroes and saints of their families, always being expected to do good deeds for others and not expected to have needs of their own. Some clergy have been in emotionally incestuous relationships with one or both parents. Emotional incest occurs when the parent comes to expect that the child will take care of his or her needs. The child stops being a child and assumes an adult role.

When this has been the case for sexually addicted clergy, we have found that their anger about being lonely and isolated is heard in the words of two of Carne's core beliefs of sex addicts, "No one likes me as I am," and "No one will take care of me but me." There develops from these core beliefs, a sense of entitlement, "I deserve to get some of my needs met." When the core belief that sex is equal to love is added to this feeling of entitlement, the belief that sexual activity will meet emotional needs develops. When someone comes along, including members of the congregation, that would do anything, even sexual activity, to please his or her pastor, a very dangerous and explosive situation develops.

Sex addicts, like all addicts, may suffer from cross addictions. Carnes discovered that 42 percent of sex addicts were also addicted to chemicals, 38 percent to eating, 28 percent to working, and 26 percent to spending.[16] Many sexually addicted pastors that we have known, for example, try to use compulsive work as a way of compensating for their sexual behavior.

It is certainly possible to assess for sexual addiction early in the life of a person who suffers from it.[17] Most sex addicts can trace their problems at least back to adolescence if not earlier. Mark Laaser, a recovering sex addict, recalls being on fire with sexual thoughts and a chronic habit of pornography usage and masturbation even in the seminary. It would have been possible to diagnosis this. Hindsight is always easier, but he believes that if he had been educated about sexual addiction, he might have been able to ask for help, even at that time.

If candidates for ministry with characteristics of sexual addiction are identified while they are in school or internships, or later in ministry, they ought to be immediately guided to get the kind of help they need. In some cases, a formal intervention may be necessary. Effective counseling resources, twelve-step fellowships, and treatment options for sexual addiction are available.[18]

Sobriety is certainly possible although like any addiction, sexual addiction is a lifetime problem. There are many sex addicts who are achieving ongoing sobriety. The serenity, joy and peace that a recovering sex addict can experience is indeed very profound. We know hundreds of examples in which lives have been changed, marriages restored, and fulfillment achieved. This is not to say that sex addicts will not experience some consequences of their addiction. But almost always, they are much better off in recovery than in their previous life.[19]

---

[16]Ibid., 35.

[17]Pat Carnes has developed two diagnostic instruments for assessing sexual addiction, the *Sexual Addiction Inventory (SAI)* and the *Sexual Addiction Screening Test (SAST)*.

[18]See the resource section in Mark Laaser's book *Faithful and True*. Cf. also the resources from the Interfaith Sexual Trauma Institute, 1-800-OSB-ISTI (672-4784).

[19]For a more detailed explanation of the process of recovery, see part 2 of Pat Carnes' book *Don't Call It Love*.

In summary, this chapter has demonstrated the wide diversity of diagnostic categories and types of issues. It is not hard to understand why those who have sought to find a psychometric method of preventing potential offenders from entering ministry have been frustrated. At best the spectrum suggests what makes a person vulnerable to sexual offending. There are certain psychological clues that we can diagnose that even in seminary predispose a person to problems with their sexuality and possible offending. Narcissistic personality disorders, antisocial disorders, obsessive compulsive disorders, the presence of sexual addiction, and other addictions may all be indicators of danger and need to be dealt with. The largest challenge remains: that of getting the student to act on our suggestion that they may need help.

This variety of psychological conditions will also need to be understood in terms of their roots in people's familial and personal lives. Our next chapter will address the etiology of those who are prone to commit sexual misconduct or offense.

# Chapter Three

# Personal Etiology of Clergy Sexual Misconduct

We have thus far described the characteristics of various types of clergy sexual offense and misconduct. The spectrum of these types suggests a broad range of psychological problems. We believe that the etiology of these problems is also complex, but that it can be traced to very significant etiological factors, including early life trauma or neglect and to the neurochemistry of the person who commits sexual misconduct or offense. This is not to say that such factors give us *all* the answers concerning sexual misconduct since everyone makes choices in the "now" of their lives, and to remain offense-free, all of us need to take responsibility in the *present* for our attitudes and actions. Our model of sexual misconduct and offense also reminds us that these etiological facts are also influenced by environment and the vulnerability of the victim. There remains, however, the fact that each choice, each responsible act, is taken under the influence of one's own personal formation and all its facets and by the chemistry in one's own brain.

## Family of Origin and Development

We believe that family systems theory is helpful in understanding the etiological issues. We agree with Michael P. Nichols who says that we seriously err unless we keep both family systems thinking *and* individual responsibility in creative tension. Family members remain separate individuals. While the system is not the absolute determinant of behavior, we do know that individuals interact within a family system in fairly predictable ways.[1] It is our conviction that looking at both individual responsibility and the person's family of origin is the most fruitful path of study.

Often people have focused on the problem of clergy sexual misconduct as a matter of ethical boundary violations. We feel that offenders, particularly, come from families where their own sense of individual identity, and therefore their ability to respect their own personal boundaries and those of others, have been significantly impaired. In this chapter we would like to present a model of how we think this happens.

The developmental damage to an individual created by early life trauma creates an inability to experience love and nurture. Those who commit sexual misconduct are often starved for love. G. K. Chesterton has been quoted as saying: "A man who knocks on the door of a brothel is knocking for God." Our experience with numerous male sex addicts would suggest that the act of soliciting prostitutes is often a desperate search for "the mother." Likewise, numerous conversations with female sex addicts would indicate that the affairs that they have had are a desperate search for "the father." One particular female addict claimed to us that in every one of the five hundred affairs she had, she was hoping that she would find in a man the love and nurture that her father did not give her.

When Jesus talked to the woman at the well he confronted a woman who had been involved with a number of men. He somehow knew that this involvement was about a thirst for love. He used this thirst to introduce her to "living water." Jesus reframed her thirst, and pointed her to more thirst-quenching permanence in a relationship with God (John 4).

We believe that it is an inherent part of human nature to search for love and connection with others. Our psychological development from infancy is built around that characteristic. Theologically, we believe that the whole process reflects the face-to-face nature of our being created for communion with God and each other. This is the foundation of both our sexuality and human community.

[1]Michael Nichols, *The Self in the System* (New York: Brunner/Mazel, 1987).

If we posit, to begin with, that being created in the image of God to seek and enjoy close communion is a basic human quality and that our psychological development from infancy is built around that characteristic, we identify a helpful theological principle. This points toward the reality that our spiritual life is bound closely to our psychological development. Divine purpose and the most powerful human drives encounter each other at the point of our capacity to love and be loved. We need to be clear, however, that communion with human beings (especially that of our family of origin) builds a foundation for our ability to commune with God, even though in terms of theological platform, the ability to relate to God is in some sense *a priori*.

John Townsend has portrayed this theological/psychological dynamic quite well in his book *Hiding from Love*. He argues that:

> We need attachment. Our ability to attach is our ability to relate our spiritual and emotional needs to others. The key word here is "relate." To relate our needs to others is to connect, or expose ourselves to them. Attachment means letting others inside the private, vulnerable parts of ourselves. . . . Attachment, or bondedness, is our deepest need. This is because it is also the deepest part of the character of God. . . . God is pro-relationship and anti-isolation.[2]

He describes other accompanying truths that influence us: (1) we are unfinished people, and (2) we fear the very things we need to restore us. "When we hide in isolation, we get worse. When we find an environment of safe relationships in order to come out from hiding, we get better. Our spiritual hunger is part of this, and so it relates both to God and others."[3] Thus, the theological and the psychological are deeply linked.

Is it not the nature of sin that we seek to satisfy this basic design by substituting our own solutions for it? Critical to our theory concerning clergy sexual misconduct is the idea that sex can be substituted for communion with God and with others.

While we are all sinful beings, and at times, are guilty of these kinds of substitutions, persons who commit clergy sexual misconduct are obviously more vulnerable to this kind of substitution of

---

[2] John Townsend, *Hiding from Love* (Colorado Springs, Colo.: Navigator Press, 1991) 62–3.

[3] Ibid., 32.

sex for communion. Where does this vulnerability come from? We believe that a person's ability to find both transcendent and interpersonal community is either facilitated or impaired by the community experience of their own family.

Inherent in our theory is a definition of boundaries. Boundaries are a way of describing our consciousness concerning personal identity and space. We can often feel uncomfortable, for example, when someone "invades our space." This sense of individual "turf" and need for control of our own safety and identity make up the boundary of our being. This boundary includes the many aspects of how we distinguish ourselves from others, including physical, emotional, social, sexual, and spiritual identity. Our boundary sense also can, under certain circumstances, include someone else, to some degree, especially that sense of who we are in a marriage, family, group, club, or church.

Where do we first start learning these boundaries? Most developmental theorists would contend that this is the task of infancy. All later development is based on how well we accomplish the task of individuation. This task is repeated cyclically throughout the various stages of life since we periodically need to develop our sense of identity in contrast to other people at each major stage of our maturation. When an eighteen-year-old is in the process of leaving home, that person needs to have discovered how to distinguish herself very clearly from her mother and father, and her own peers to a sufficient degree that she can make clear and defined choices for herself. Her ability to do this will be based on the successful completion of her individuation at earlier stages of her life and her competence to stretch that development now in positive forward movement. Some of us come from families which either facilitate this individuation process or impair it in a variety of ways.

## The Circumplex Model and Sexuality[4]

In family we find out who we are and how to be identified as an individual; we also learn how to perceive and respect the

[4]David H. Olson, Candice S. Russell, Douglas H. Sprenkle, eds., *Circumplex Model: Systemic Assessment and Treatment of Families* (New York: Haworth Press, 1989).

boundaries of other persons. It is now a well-known feature of family studies that there is a continuum of types of family structures.[5] In tightly enmeshed families, the "boundary skin" of the other person is seen as more permeable, more subject to being under the influence of others in the family system. In such a family, for example, it might not be seen as intrusive to make comments about another family member in their presence which would be taken as intrusive in a less enmeshed system. Therefore, in the more tightly-knit family type, it is sometimes difficult to know where one's own boundaries stop and others' boundaries begin—thus, confusion about boundaries results. Add emotional or physical abuse, or in extreme cases, incest, and we see even more boundary confusion.

In extremely disengaged families the individual is encouraged to operate in more solitary ways. With disengaged family settings the isolation may create deep longings for closeness that cannot be obtained. Questions may arise about one's loveability. With those questions there may be present a good deal of anger and periodic inappropriate behavior.

To increase the mix, when we change the nuclear family in some way, either through divorce, or change of unmarried parental partners, the confusion about boundaries increases. Add to this element the trauma of loss and grief in such situations, and we have developing for children greater potential for experiencing misuse of our power later on in their adulthood, either as perpetrators or as victims. Perpetrators cross boundaries either out of frustrated need for connectedness or out of inadequate perception of the boundaries of victims, or both. We will need to think of ways to re-orient people concerning proper respect for boundaries in order to do good preventive education.

Whatever the style of the family, it seems that there will be the possibility that an individual will be intrusively invaded, neglectfully abandoned, or both. James Maddock, for example, describes one unhealthy extreme as a sexually abusive family, and another as sexually neglectful. The neglectful family ignores members' sexuality except perhaps in the marital relationship.

[5]David H. Olson and others, "Circumplex Model of Marital and Family Systems: VI: Theoretical Update," *Family Process* 22, 62–93.

Family members, especially the children, get little opportunity to test sexual reality in this system. Affection and physical touch may be lacking. Children may have reason to doubt how loved they are. The opposite type, the abusive family, is usually tightly closed, undifferentiated, and rigid. Sexualized dependency is the norm. Invasiveness of one's boundaries would be more frequent. In many families, the potential for both forms of boundary problems exists. For example, we look at the classically incestuous family, in which one parent is perpetrating sexual trauma on a child, and the other parent is failing to provide protection from invasion.[6]

Maddock describes a sexually healthy family as one where both the individual identity and the integrity of the family system are maintained at the same time, with a balance of influence between males and females. Boundaries are respected between the sexes, but nevertheless there is ample opportunity to talk appropriately about sexual issues at each developmental stage. Developmentally appropriate values are held for sexuality. Members of these families experience positive forms of touch and physical interaction, without emotional or physical invasiveness.

Patrick Carnes, a well-known addictionologist who specializes in sexual issues, has identified sex addicts as often coming from extreme family types, whether those that neglect the emotional needs of the child, on the one hand, or invade the space and privacy of the child, on the other. With a survey of 289 sexual addicts he discovered that 78 percent of them identified their families of origin as rigid. These families put high priority on doing things right, being judgmental, and disapproving of anything sexual. They were also disengaged (87 percent), with little care taken for the feelings of the child, easily developing a conditional love that fostered a strong sense of toxic shame and unworthiness. "These families operate with detachment and distance, with low affirmation and approval, and with high levels of criticism and disapproval."[7]

[6]James W. Maddock, "Healthy Family Sexuality: Positive Principles for Educators and Clinicians," *Family Relations* 38, 130–6.
[7]Patrick Carnes, *Don't Call It Love: Recovery from Sexual Addiction* (New York: Bantam Books, 1991) 101.

Carnes goes on to identify these families as having their toughest battles over boundaries since parents in these families believe sincerely that "kids don't have rights" and force kids to do things that do not feel good or safe. "These children's boundaries become permeable. They grow up feeling that they have to give whatever is asked: explanations, help, information—and sex."[8] Carnes states that only 2.5 percent of his sample of addicts came from normal "healthy" range on the circumplex model, whereas two-thirds come from families that were both rigid and disengaged.[9]

In summary, either invading or abandoning a person's boundaries leave long-lasting wounds for the individual. If we divide a person into four dimensions: emotional, physical, sexual, and spiritual, we can see that acts of abandonment or invasion can occur in each of those dimension.[10] Carnes discovered, for example, in a study with over two thousand sex addicts, that 97 percent reported trauma in the emotional dimension, 74 percent in the physical dimension, and 81 percent in the sexual dimension.[11]

|  | Emotional | Physical | Sexual | Spiritual |
|---|---|---|---|---|
| Invasion |  |  |  |  |
| Abandonment |  |  |  |  |

*Figure 2*

## Developmental Issues

When we observe the developing infant in psychological terms, as Margaret Mahler and others have done, it is not difficult to identify the basic need for a unified relationship experience of elements such as nurture, acceptance, communion and social support. To look back to our most primitive individual memories is to see that being enfolded in loving arms, to nuzzle a nourishing warm breast, to feel totally cared for, and satisfied with that

[8]Ibid., 102.
[9]Ibid., 106.
[10]For a lengthier explanation of ways in which abuse is perpetrated, see Mark Laaser, *Faithful and True* (Grand Rapids, Mich.: Zondervan Publications, 1996) 100.
[11]Ibid., n. 7.

care, is a set of foundational building blocks of health and well-being. Add to this the ability to look into responsively loving eyes of the parent and to be able to do that frequently enough to have reassurance of our being valued and observed in caring ways. The stage we are in transmutes the way we experience these basic elements to some extent, but they remain central and vital to our health and ability to extend ourselves into the unknown as we mature toward individuality and a sense of competence.[12]

More to the point in terms of assessing candidates for ministry, given the high incidence of problematic families of origin, the process of development for many has been one of insufficient nurture and affection. Healthy levels of interpersonal intimacy have often not developed. These people are working with serious deficits, but they may not have recognized this clearly and consciously for themselves. They know only that they long for some indefinable experience that will fill the empty hollows of their emotional self. In short, they long for love and nurture, closeness, and comfort.

Along with this, goes the issue of one's inner assessment of competence in the basic areas of life, such as intersex friendship—the ability to see oneself as both attractive to, and comfortable with, the opposite sex. To the developing psyche, such potential friends are attractive and represent something desirable but unobtainable since they do not feel competent to relate. If this self-assessment is predominantly negative, there may develop a sense of anger against persons of the opposite sex. The inner dialog for the male might go something like this:

> She has the "treasure" I want, but I can't have it; There's probably more to this than sex, but I can easily define sex as "the something" that excites me. I'm angry that I don't have the interpersonal skill to get her to give that mysterious "something" to me. So, I'll just overwhelm her, and take it.

A man's view of women is critical here. If a woman is seen as possessing "the treasure" of nurture and support we long for, she

---

[12]Margaret S. Mahler and Fred Pine, *The Psychological Birth of the Human Infant* (New York: Basic Books, 1975).

can either be portrayed as the pedestal "exalted virgin" or the "degraded whore" whose evil power over us is to be simultaneously feared or attacked. Our attitude toward her largely determines our actions. In addictionology circles, the root of the problem is often named "love hunger" (Carnes). We do not affirm here that all sexual misconduct can be traced to an addiction. However, addictions illustrate some basic elements of what happens in many, if not most people's inner life. Greg Nakken describes an addicted person as one who attempts to substitute intensity for intimacy. By this he means that instead of seeking appropriate ways to develop our intimate connectedness and nurture, addicted persons seek to fill that need by using short-cuts to feeling good about themselves by using chemicals, taking adrenaline-rush types of risk, or through relationships that are abusively weighted in favor of the addicted person's needs being met in some substitutionary way.[13]

Ideally, the "love hunger" should be satisfied by mutually nurturing relationships that are respectful and supportive, that fill us with that satisfying sense of well-being and satisfaction with self and others. Along with this should goes an increasingly mature ability to sacrifice for the sake of others, to serve, to give, to stretch in behalf of the good of the whole social group.

The well-known Austrian psychologist Alfred Adler described a healthy person using a complex German word *(Gemeindschaftsgefuehl)* Literally this means a feeling for society; more broadly it denotes "a sensitivity to the whole social fabric." This comes close to the New Testament concept of *agape*-love, a love that unselfishly seeks the good of the other. In contrast, immature, selfish love is such that in certain cases it attempts to conquer, thus ruling out genuinely and mutually beneficial relationships. (It is notable that in Latin America, the term *conquista* [conquest] is often used to describe relationships with females.) Our use of power, therefore, is bound up in this whole process of seeking what we need. Adler linked healthy personality development to a sense of personal potency. White called this "competence."

---

[13]Greg Nakken, *The Addictive Personality* (Center City, Minn.: Hazelden Publications, 1986).

However, until we understand how competence and love are related in our seeking of intimacy, particularly in healthy mutual sexuality, we have not solved our problem of understanding the way people cross sexual boundaries inappropriately.

Though it belongs most clearly to another realm of our model, the issue of power obviously is relevant here because individuals develop within systems and are influenced in their individuality by those systems. Males in our culture often possess both the physical strength and the social status to exercise disproportionate power over females. If the love deficits we described are present, as well as the negative self-assessment, there is a strong temptation to abuse one's physical strength and social potency and forcefully (or blindly) cross women's personal boundaries to obtain the answers to the male's needs. The need to dominate females could often be traced back to the basic need for both nurture and acceptance. Because of deficits in the male's own development, therefore, there is a drive to misuse power.

One experienced military chaplain who had intervened on several cases of clergy sexual misconduct in his work setting told us that, oddly enough, almost all the chaplain perpetrators he had interviewed described themselves as feeling powerless and impotent. In our need to overcome our impotency, and in our anxious search to get close to others, we push through the boundaries, not always aware of the damage we are doing in the process. Males who have not learned loving respect for others will assume an available role or utilize any social device they can come up with to attempt to fulfill their longing. That is why the boundaries need reinforcement through ethical and social sanctions. However, we may be able to "cut this off at the pass" by teaching seminarians about these dynamics and alerting them to their own potential for harm.

Gordon Benson, in his doctoral research for Boston University, found that all the subjects in his sample of clergy sexual offenders told stories of being emotionally abandoned by a parent or parent surrogate.[14]

---

[14]Gordon L. Benson, "Sexual Behavior by Male Clergy with Adult Female Counselees: Systemic and Situational Themes," *Sexual Addiction and Compulsivity* (1994) 1:2, 103–18.

There are obvious religious components involved in the construction of values and understandings of family. Seminarians who can delve into how the spiritual and theological values of their family system were learned, expressed, and reinforced will gain much insight into what needs adjustment in their adulthood for a healthier functioning of their own sexuality and interpersonal closeness.

From this discussion of families and our learning about boundaries, therefore, we can conclude that seminarians need to examine their family of origin in order to understand what family forces are there to shape their attitudes toward sexual boundaries as well as healthy or unhealthy ideas about true intimacy. We will need to preventively facilitate a healing of early life trauma in the formation process of candidates for ministry. This healing will enable completion of early developmental tasks that have previously been impaired.

## Sexualizing Our Need for Nurture

There is enough data about the ways families function to safely hypothesize that people who sexualize their need for nurture come from family settings where there is not enough caring, safe touch, or affection, nor appropriate closeness mixed with respect for individual boundaries. Patrick Carnes' research mentioned above certainly reinforces such an idea.

In our culture great attention is given by the advertising and entertainment media to sexualizing every "meaningful encounter" and ignoring the long-term features of building a good friendship base. One does not have to watch television very long to notice the almost total absence of focus upon careful preparation of a marriage relationship and the gradual and challenging work of creating the right conditions of a home for the arrival of a child.

It would appear to be imperative that seminaries include course work and discussion of healthy sexuality and family of origin issues. Just as fifth-grade children are being taught to resist drug and alcohol abuse by police officers (D.A.R.E.), seminarians need to be taught to aim at healthy intimacy skills and values for building homes where people are nurtured, developed, and launched in optimal conditions. They need these skills themselves, and they need to be able to teach them to others in the congregations where they will serve.

## Neurochemistry

It is not within the scope of our expertise to explore a field, neurochemistry, which is in its infancy. It is impossible to ignore, however, that neurophysiologists are beginning to give us clues about predisposition to mental health disorders and addictive disease, and conversely how behaviors effect neurophysiology.

We have found the work of Milkman and Sunderwirth to be particularly helpful in understanding the relationship of a person's brain chemistry to mental health and addictive disease.[15] In a recent article they have explored the direct relationship of neurochemistry to sexual addiction.[16] They contend that sexual fantasy and/or activity creates neurochemical reactions in the reward centers of the brain that are identical to those created by cocaine. The tolerance that the brain builds to these neurochemical changes is also similar. The tolerance factor leads addicts to needing more and more of the same activity or to new and more "exciting" activity to achieve the same effect. This phenomenon lends credence to a sex addict's feeling that his or her addiction is no different than a drug addiction.

Neurophysiological factors such as this one can create a need for more and more dangerous and exciting behaviors. Sexual offending behaviors can become an escalating pattern of increasingly serious activities as a sexually addicted perpetrator searches for ongoing maintenance of the neurochemical "high." Thorough neurological and psychiatric evaluation of sexual offenders has become a clinical necessity. Doing such evaluations with candidates for ministry is difficult to demand and expensive and arduous to achieve, but it may be necessary if other risk factors are present, particularly a history of sexual offending behavior.

---

[15]Harvey Milkman and Stan Sunderwirth, *Craving for Ecstasy* (Lexington, Mass.: Lexington Books).

[16]Harvey Milkman and others, "Neurochemistry and Sexual Addiction," *Sexual Addiction and Compulsivity* (1996) 3:1, 22–32.

This chapter has attempted to portray the various possible sources of a person's tendency to transgress other people's boundaries, including traumas or abandonment in their family of origin, the sexualization of the need for nurture, or the physical-neurological make-up of the body. In the following two chapters we will continue to explore our model of the sexually offending moment and deal with environmental factors and the nature of victim's issues. While it is always easier and more "black and white" to focus on the dynamics of an offender, the broader picture always needs to remain in focus.

# Chapter Four

# Environmental Factors

In this chapter we will examine environmental factors that contribute to acts of clergy sexual misconduct. In certain unhealthy environmental conditions even the healthiest of individuals may succumb to sexual misconduct. Conversely, there will be unhealthy individuals who sexually act out in the healthiest of environments. Our understanding of environment is a broad one. It includes several dimensions outside of an individual. These include the cultural and theological, social, and physical environments.

## Culture and Theology

Cultural and theological beliefs are important as an environmental dimension because of the way they define attitudes about men, women, relationships, roles, power, and sexuality. These attitudes will affect the way the people behave toward each other, including respecting each other's integrity and boundaries. Culturally and theologically defined attitudes and beliefs will also affect how people symbolize love, sex, and power. A pastor, for example, might admit to having a "mutual affair" with a member of his congregation and that this included "making love" to her. This pastor may seek to justify the relationship by believing he really cared for the woman. However, current ethical and legal understanding is that this pastor used his superior emotional and spiritual power to sexually exploit this woman, that there was nothing mutual about it, and that the consequences will ultimately be devastating to the woman.

When men in power sexually abuse women, attitudes that can contribute to this are male-oriented and male-dominated. They hold that men are superior to women and more able to be in positions of power. This orientation allows men who are preoccupied with their own insecurities to use power over women to give them a sense of worth. All too often gaining sexual access is a way of testing whether one has power over women. Women who seek equal power will run full force into these well defended bastions of male insecurity and power. The resulting power struggles create damaging anger and resentment. We have known women in positions of power, including female clergy, who have acted out sexually with men under their power. This situation, too, can indicate a search for equal power through sex.

Male clergy have struggled to accept this critique, but too often they slip right back into the comfort of their traditional roles and beliefs. It is always more psychologically comfortable to retain what is familiar. This was driven home to one of us while teaching an egalitarian view of Ephesians 5 in a seminary classroom. After the exposition, replete with Greek clauses and exegetical comments, an obviously threatened seminarian retorted loudly: "Professor, I'm deeply disappointed in you!" To see that passage, or others such as 1 Corinthians 11.3-16 or 1 Timothy 2:11-15 as culturally conditioned, is too frightening to many males. This reflects the male-dominant cultural environment from which they come.[1]

Most religious bodies have come under criticism for these attitudes from inside their own ranks. In Roman Catholic circles, for example, the critiques leveled by A. W. Richard Sipe at the belief system and practice concerning women has not been well received. One of his main arguments is that many Roman Catholic writings portray women, on the one hand, as "evil temptresses," and on the other exalt them to a pedestal. There exists an "Eve-the-Seductress vs. Virgin Mary" ambivalence, combined with a

---

[1]Cf. the excellent survey and exposition of the issues in Stanley J. Grenz and Denise Muir Kjesbo, *Women in the Church: A Biblical Theology of Women in Ministry* (Downers Grove, Ill.: InterVarsity Press, 1995).

dualistic view of sexuality. This results, he believes, in the exalta-tion of male celibates over "inferior women."[2]

In conservative evangelical circles we frequently find a similar reticence concerning ordination and full certification of the spir-itual gifts of women. At one ordination council where a woman candidate was being examined, and one of us was in attendance, several Baptist men pushed her hard to explain her beliefs con-cerning 1 Timothy 3:13-14: "For Adam was formed first, then Eve. And Adam was not the one deceived; it was the woman who was deceived and became a sinner." It became obvious early in the discussion that these male clergy felt that these verses dis-qualified her from ordination to the ministry. This disqualifica-tion often contains the culturally-shaped assumption that women are inferior by both creation and the fall.

Certainly it is not correct to say that only those churches that refuse to ordain women need to examine the issue of their view of women in ministry. What one author has called "the stained glass ceiling" exists in most mainline denominations that ordain women. We face the difficult task of changing the whole culture, rather than one or another denominational structure.

Another critical feature of the cultural scene is how a demean-ing view of women influences the way we help hurting women. Starting with our language about women counselees (e.g., jokes about PMS and menopause, "hysterics," and "hypochondriacal woman"), we need to examine and mature our treatment of women. Obviously, with the history of woman's place in society being what it is, more women are dependent upon males, and act dependently with male clergy.

In some churches personality cults are enhanced by an expec-tation that a strong, charismatic personality is needed to galva-nize and lead a church. When we combine this mind-set with a lower view of women than is due them, both theologically and socially, we set ourselves up for abusing them.

Feminist writers in the arena of violence toward women chal-lenge males to ask themselves: "Would I hit a male for the same

---

[2]A. W. Richard Sipe, *A Secret World: Sexuality and the Search for Celibacy* (New York: Brunner/Mazel, 1990). Also, *Sex, Priests and Power: Anatomy of a Crisis* (New York: Brunner/Mazel, 1995).

level of provocation for which I hit a woman?" In like manner, prospective or active male clergy need to ask: "Would I treat a male helper with the same 'discounts' that I apply to a woman in the same circumstances?" Our culture sets us up for certain mismanagement in the area of our sexuality.

Men are expected to be more focused on genital sex, more needy in terms of sexual gratification, and to take a more aggressive stance toward women than vice versa. Women are often told that "pleasing men, catching men, and holding them in a relationship will mean that they use their wiles." Men are seen to be in a power-position; women have less power. Thus, when we look at the clergy-client situation in which clergy are usually males and clients often women, that whole cultural baggage comes with the picture. Peter Rutter, the well-known author of *Sex in The Forbidden Zone,* in an interview by Lewis Rambo, comments on the distressing reality: "Many women don't even perceive boundary violations because they've accepted [them] as the standard way society works."[3]

Another aspect of this negative systemic attitude is that women who want and need help from male clergy too often these days meet up with men who are fearful because of all the clergy sexual misconduct cases. Women are considered inimical to clergy because at the slightest cause they will sue or bring charges. Women have told us that when they sought counseling from a pastor, they are treated like "moral lepers" or "The Dangerous Woman." Again, the message is one that blames the victim, and male clergy need to check and correct such attitudes.

Another recent cultural symptom of the historical imbalance of power between men and women is the increased awareness of sexual harassment. Many businesses and industries are facing lawsuits. As women search for equal power in the workplace, sexual tensions have become more openly revealed. Likewise, the growing number of women who have sought ordination have begun to expose the amount of sexual harassment and abuse that they suffered at the hands of male professors, supervisors, and ecclesiastical superiors. Our experience in talking with female candidates

[3]Lewis Rambo, "Interview with Dr. Peter Rutter, Author of *Sex in the Forbidden Zone,* July 27, 1990," *Pastoral Psychology* (1991) 39:5, 321–33.

for ministry indicates how common and pervasive this problem is. These cases point to the fact that as women have sought equal power in ministry, men have continued to search for continuing control of women by sexually objectifying and manipulating them. There is no doubt that these struggles have contributed to a level of environmental sexual tension that cannot be denied in many situations.

James Poling, in his book *The Abuse of Power*, said that cultural systems can create power imbalances that may not protect the vulnerable:

> Society dictates how power is distributed. Institutions and ideologies determine who has privilege to be dominant and who must defer. Some persons are given great power to make choices for themselves and other people and are protected from the consequences of their choices. But many are denied the power to control even their own bodies and minds, and their choices are circumscribed by others. These inequities create the occasions for abusive behaviors and unjust power arrangements. Religion serves to define the nature of power and its legitimate uses. Religious leaders must choose whether to collude with the dominant culture as sanctioning agents of abusive power or to be prophetic critics of the way power is distributed and defined. Sexual violence can serve as a test for understanding the nature of power and its destructive and creative potential in an unjust society.[4]

Poling takes the issue to theological lengths that we would not subscribe to, with severe modification of long-standing orthodoxy. We do agree, however, with his call for careful examination of all the ways in which world view and theology contribute to harmful or disrespectful treatment by males of women and children.

Marie Fortune, Joy Jordan-Lake, Mary Pellauer, Karen Labacqz, and Pamela Cooper-White, among others, have all written articles and books concerning the ethical guidelines which need to be in place for a system to function without harming the vulnerable.[5] To lead is to be responsible for the ethical and moral

---

[4]James N. Poling, *The Abuse of Power: A Theological Problem* (Nashville: Abingdon Press, 1991) 12–3.

[5]Marie Fortune, *Is Nothing Sacred? When Sex Invades the Pastoral Relationship* (New York: Harper and Row, 1989). Joy Jodan-Lake, "Conduct Unbecoming a

features of the system we lead. Marilyn R. Peterson's excellent book *At Personal Risk*[6] states that boundaries in professional-client relationships are there for the safety and well-being of the client. Lay leaders and clergy are together called to make sure that ethical guidelines are followed for the safety of everyone under their care.

Lloyd Rediger has also written on cultural and theological attitudes in his book on sexuality in ministry. He identifies a systemic factor within the culture of the church system which he calls the "Star Factor":

> Ministry elevates males to a position of influence and dominance far above their peers. The term "star" describes the unique combination of being the identified spiritual leader of a congregation, a recognizable moral leader in the community, and a performer in the spotlight leading people in their liturgical worship of God. This is heady—even in an increasingly secularized society. No other profession offers an individual the responsibility of standing in front of an audience at least once every week and interpreting God, life, and morality for them. No amount of humility, denial, or self-effacement can alter the immense stimulation and satisfaction derived from this regular opportunity.[7]

Such standing and power has a centuries-long precedent, and easily transposes cultural lines. Few people have the spiritual, psychological, and emotional maturity to handle this well. Once we add the mystique of spiritual intimacy with God that often accompanies this role, and physical attractiveness and a caring personal style in ministers, the stage is set to draw needy people to male clergy, including women. Rediger poignantly states the

---

Pastor," *Christianity Today* (February 10, 1992) 26–30. Mary Pellauer and others, eds., *Sexual Assault and Abuse: A Handbook for Clergy and Religious Professionals* (New York: Harper and Row, 1987). Also, "Sex, Power, and the Family of God: Clergy and Sexual Abuse in Counseling," *Christianity and Crisis* (1987) 47, 47–50. Karen Labacqz and Ronald G. Barton, *Sex in the Parish* (Louisville: Westminster/John Knox Press, 1991). Pamela Cooper-White, "Soul Stealing: Power Relations in Pastoral Sexual Abuse," *The Christian Century* (1991) 108, 196–9.

[6]Marilyn R. Peterson, *At Personal Risk* (New York: W. W. Norton, 1992).

[7]Lloyd Rediger, *Ministry and Sexuality* (Minneapolis: Augsburg Publishing, 1990) 15.

problem: "The star factor contributes significantly to clergy sexual malfeasance by blinding the performer and the admiring observer to the realities of meaningful, responsible relationships."[8] Church and pastor(s) should face the reality of this tempting situation together and continually be alert to its manifestations and implications.

However, in contrast to the above, some observers of church life have noted an increase in the number of churches where clergy are increasingly under attack by, and more isolated from, congregational leaders. This feature further stresses the minister's ability to be nurtured within the church system itself and remain healthy. Thus, there may be an increasing tendency for such ministers to seek sexual expressions of love and support.

There are other cultural and theological factors that contribute to the possibility of sexual misconduct other than the male-oriented attitudes and beliefs which may contribute to abuse of women by men. The sexual revolution of the 1960s and 1970s has also left culture rather morally adrift, bereft of solid cultural values concerning sexual morality. The baby-boom generation turned from what they perceived to be hypocritical moral values to free love. The sexual revolution may have freed up some historical sexual inhibitions and worn out taboos, but it has also created a variety of indications of moral decay. The divorce rate, incidence of unwed pregnancies, and the increase of sexually transmitted diseases are only a few of these symptoms.

Environmentally, we believe that there has been a dramatic increase in the number of sexual stimuli as a result of the sexual revolution. While pornography has always existed, for example, it is much more readily available today than it was twenty-five years ago. Our advertising media depend on sex appeal to sell products. The movies, television, music, and magazines are full of sexual content. Today it is impossible to avoid sexual stimuli in the most common places. Imagine, for example, checking out of the grocery story and not being bombarded with images and messages with sexual content in the magazines that are always sold there.

[8]Ibid., 18.

Most of us have been so desensitized to these stimuli that we do not focus on the messages about sex that they convey to us. A few that come to mind are: that sex and love are synonymous, that when we are being sexual we are making love; that sex is a certain unalienable right, i.e., we all deserve to be involved; sex is recreational, something to be enjoyed even after the first date; sex is never dangerous or leads to consequences; sex is always romantic and exciting; and the more partners that you experience in life, the happier you will be. The result of all these messages, sometimes unconsciously conveyed, is that many of us feel rather left out, unworthy, or unattractive if we are not involved.

A dangerous list of beliefs can emerge from these cultural and theological influences:

1. Women are inferior to men and should not be in power. They are weak and vulnerable and should be cared for in a controlling way.
2. One way to control another person is through the yeses and nos of sexual activity.
3. Sexual involvement is an indication of attractiveness and worth.
4. Sex is for everyone and no one will get hurt.
5. Sex is equal to love. Caring for someone else means that sex is always an expression of that caring.

Even a candidate for ministry who is healthy emotionally and spiritually might succumb to one or more of these beliefs. To the degree that this is the case, the door opens to the possibility of sexual misconduct.

## Social Factors That Contribute to Sexual Misconduct

Jeff Seat and his colleagues have identified a set of social factors that may contribute to sexual misconduct. Systemically, he studied the stress level a system places upon clergy, and personally, the adequacy of the training received to deal with ministry. Seat's study examined questionnaires from 277 Southern Baptist pastors in six southern states. He noted the reported incidence of sexual misconduct among them (slightly higher than for clinical psychologists) and correlated this with their stress level. He concludes: "Now it appears that stress plays a critical role in not only the physical and emotional health of the ministers but also their behavioral health as well."[9] From this we conclude that church leadership and seminaries need to be alert to the need for stress management and self-care issues, as well as to thoroughly educate prospective clergy about these needs. As Seat and his colleagues point out: "The difficulty is compounded in the Southern Baptist denomination by the denial factor and the lack of an appropriate forum for the expression of problems."[10] The Southern Baptist Convention is certainly not alone in this regard!

Rev. Gordon MacDonald, in his book *Rebuilding Your Broken World*, describes some of the personal and social issues involved in clergy misconduct. He himself carried on a secret sexual liaison while pastoring a thriving church in Massachusetts, while also writing best-selling books, and while speaking in conferences across the country. He says that weariness, personal depletion, adversity and frustration, grief, loss, anger, stress, can all be part of the church system that pastors allow to become dysfunctional and impairing features of their personal lives. He pleads with other pastors to not allow themselves to work in situations like this without taking care of themselves, being accountable to supportive, responsible friends and colleagues. Pastors must take responsibility for the effects of systems upon their personal lives and make choices that enable them to be healthy and stay healthy in every area of their lives.[11]

It appears from MacDonald's account, veiled as it is concerning how and why he fell into problems in his own case, that his fall was due to failure to observe the effects of all the stresses in his own life coupled with the lack of a good external "reality check." The church system in which he worked probably did not have built into it any kinds of checks and balances to preserve the health of the minister while also keeping ministerial power under reasonable scrutiny. In most cases this kind of setting, combined with

[9]Jeff T. Seat and others, "The Prevalence and Contributing Factors of Sexual Misconduct among Southern Baptist Pastors in Six Southern States," *Journal of Pastoral Care* (Winter 1993) 363–72.

[10]Ibid., 370.

[11]Gordon MacDonald, *Rebuilding Your Broken World* (Nashville: Oliver-Nelson Books, 1988).

opportunities to take advantage of needy people in order to meet one's own internal needs, is often difficult to handle successfully. William L. White has served as a consultant to treatment centers for many years and has become knowledgeable concerning the ways in which treatment center settings as systems become turned in on themselves and produce problems for employees as well as administrators and clients. When a work setting becomes chaotic, turbulent, and pressure-filled, and persons working there are called upon to give of themselves sacrificially, boundaries between persons and the corporate entity become blurred. Unless leadership people take steps to keep values and boundaries clearly defined, this organization can become what he calls "an incestuous system."

The proactive stance involves not only having good ethical guidelines in place but also taking care that people working in the system have appropriate ways to get their needs met, to stay healthy personally and professionally, and to channel their "power, anger, aggression, physical depletion, loneliness or desperate needs for self-affirmation [in ways other than] with sexual attraction."[12] Organizational leaders must model the values and habits that they promote in their corporate vision and ethical guidelines. He states that over the years he has noted many organizations that move into a mode of existence where people inside the organization unwisely attempt "to meet most if not all of their personal, professional, social and sexual needs inside the boundary of the organization."[13]

One of the most insightful descriptions White offers concerns the similarities between an incestuous family and an incestuous organization. Like families, organizations that are too preoccupied with their own internal relationships, and lack external input and interchange, easily sexualize these internal relationships.

At its worst sexual exploitation can be institutionalized as an element of the culture of a closed system. In such circumstances the abusive episodes are large in number, occur over extended

---

[12]William L. White, *Incest in the Organizational Family: The Ecology of Burnout in Closed Systems* (Bloomington, Ill.: Lighthouse Training Institute Publications, 1986).

[13]Ibid., 190.

periods of time, and involve large numbers of perpetrators and exploited clients. Sexual harassment of workers and sexual exploitation of workers often emerge out of the same abuses of power within such organizations. The high level of unmet needs and the distortion of values within the closed system put anyone interacting with this system at high risk for exploitation.[14]

It is not difficult for those of us in seminary and church leadership to recognize this phenomenon in certain churches and church organizations. Closed religious systems can be motivated by many kinds of factors, including a need to establish a comfortable "safe haven," combined with fear of the outside chaotic world. Once we combine this with the presence of people who depend upon the explicit and dogmatic guidance of an authoritarian leader who tends to make their decisions for them, we have the makings of an extremely closed and potentially abusive system.

Ronald M. Enroth, a sociologist at Westmont College, has described abusive churches as those that misuse spiritual authority, use fear, guilt, and threats to control their people, see themselves as "special," foster rigidity in their members, discourage questions, and finally, make leaving them painful.[15] Ken Blue, a San Diego pastor and author, notes that people who have shame-based backgrounds are particularly vulnerable to this kind of leadership style. They believe in a perfection-demanding God, but not in grace and renewal, and trapped in such a theology and convictions arising out of their family of origin, they are extremely vulnerable to manipulative, power-abusing clergy and church systems.[16] It is important to note that shame-based families often lie behind sexual addiction, so that shame operates both in the individual and the larger system of the church with disastrous results.

The truth is that both lay people and clergy are held under the sway of these systems. Lewis B. Smedes, in his book *Shame and Grace*, describes a pastor whom he calls "C. Prescott McCaernish,"

[14]Ibid., 191.
[15]Ronald M. Enroth, *Recovering from Churches That Abuse* (Grand Rapids, Mich.: Zondervan Publications, 1994).
[16]Ken Blue, *Healing Spiritual Abuse* (Downers Grove, Ill.: InterVarsity Press, 1993).

who grew up in the shadow of a parson-father ". . . Than whom no man could have been more acceptable." He heard from his earliest days, "Your father was a great man of God, and if you can be half the man he is, you will do well." He devoted himself to become acceptable to God and his father. He attained success as a pastor, eloquent and sacrificially hard working and self-denying. Inside, however, he was a frightened child ashamed he would never be able to become the man his father was. Smedes caps the account with an almost poetic metaphor: "He found someone who had a talent for accepting unacceptable men; she nestled him, warmed him, excited him, and accepted him. She took him in; the congregation put him out."[17]

Smedes' story is another example of how people in congregations search for the healing of the wounds they have felt since childhood. Lonely and hurting people who are searching for the love of God and each other may have come to symbolize love and nurture in unhealthy ways. If the pastor and vulnerable people in the congregation use sex as a symbol of love and nurture, or if they search for personal power through sex, the system creates an arsenal of heat seeking missiles that attract each other.

Tragically, many of the victims of pastoral sexual abuse were incest victims. These victims may be looking to the role of the male pastor as a father figure to heal a "father wound." Their experience may have been that the way to relate to a father is through sex. This is what they know. If the pastor becomes sexual with them, it is a repetition of their earlier incest and the result is re-traumatizing.[18]

There are church systems in which the pastor enjoys a powerful role as a charismatic father figure. While on the one hand the church benefits from a caring and dynamic style of leadership, on the other hand it may suffer from over dependence on the strength of this style. Members of the church who are desperate for or who are trusting of a father's attention and love will be more vulnerable to this style.

---

[17]Lewis Smedes, *Shame and Grace: Healing the Shame We Don't Deserve* (San Francisco: HarperCollins, 1993).

[18]Gerald Blanchard, "Sexually Abusive Clergymen: A Conceptual Framework for Intervention and Recovery," *Pastoral Psychology* (March 1991) 237–46.

We remember clearly two examples of these rather "incestuous" situations. In one Catholic church the priest was sexual with several adolescent boys. The members of this church considered this priest the best pastor they had ever had. Many admirers still had a hard time believing he could be guilty of misconduct. Angry members blamed the bishop for not getting him help sooner. Some even blamed the parents of the boys for not being good parents and that this led to the boys being vulnerable. It is clear that some of the parents did in fact trust the priest to be a surrogate father figure to their family.

In another situation a minister had been sexual with several women in the church. This pastor had built this church into one of the largest in the area. Some of its members refused to believe the obvious and admitted facts. In one surprising congregational meeting in which the leadership of the church was trying to explain the dismissal of the pastor, many women in the church rose to his defense, saying what a wonderful man he was. The result of these feelings was that a faction of the members left this church, formed a new one, and reinstated the dismissed pastor.

We have done some research with pastors who have followed offending pastors into the churches in which sexual misconduct was committed. The love of the offending pastor has been so strong that many of these "after pastors" have faced the anger of people who feel that he or she is trying to take the place of the one who is gone. Some of these pastors have actually left the ministry over stress from these situations.[19]

It is also clear from our research in this area that a congregation with needs for a strong, charismatic, and fathering style of leadership will find such a person and possibly recreate a incestuous environment. We know of one church, for example, in which five successive pastors were sexual with members of the congregation. Environmentally, some churches are going to be so demanding of a pastor, that even the strongest of persons may succumb to its pressures.

---

[19]Nancy Hopkins and Mark Laaser, eds., *Restoring the Soul of a Church: Healing Congregations Wounded by Clergy Sexual Misconduct* (Collegeville: The Liturgical Press, 1995).

Finally, the system of a pastor's marriage can also contribute to vulnerability to sexual misconduct. Anecdotally, we have known for some time that "problems in the parsonage" will indicate a lonely, needy, and vulnerable pastor. Some people may have even felt sorry for the poor and overworked pastor whose wife does not give him the love and attention that he so desperately deserves. It is not uncommon for a wife to be the one who suffers much of the blame in a situation of pastoral sexual misconduct. While this thinking is tragic, it is true that marital trouble is an indication of pastoral vulnerability.

Marital difficulty might be an indication of the emotional problems of the pastor and his or her spouse. These same problems on the part of a pastor may also make them vulnerable to sexual misconduct. It is also possible that marital difficulty is the result of the stress of the role of pastor and the role of pastoral spouse, both generally being overworked and under paid. Many pastoral couples have very poor boundaries concerning their time and privacy. Pastoral marriages are often ones in which there is unequal status. The pastor is admired and loved, while the spouse is ignored while expected to perform more menial and less powerful functions. This can create jealousies and resentments that can lead to marital difficulty.

Marital stress leaves some pastors tired, lonely, and needy. Sexual distance and infrequency may obviously be a part of the marital problem. Combine this factor with the access a pastor has to the lives of people in the congregation whose marriages may also be poor and the image of heat seeking missiles becomes apparent again. A lonely pastor may even think that he has not married the person who God really intended him to marry and feel "entitled" to find the right one. There are usually many in congregations who are willing to give the pastor more than what they perceive the spouse is doing. These comments raise the need for marriage enrichment courses for seminarians and pastors.

We note that in situations in which this environmental factor is combined with the pathology of the pastor (note the intersection of these two circles in our model of the offending moment), the entitlement factor can be used by the pastor as a predatory device. The alleged story of the evangelist Jim Bakker revealed that he used his role as a tired and needy man who ministered to millions of others while no one ministered to him to gain sexual access. It was almost as if being sexual with him was ministering to him so that he could minister to others.

## Physical Factors That Contribute to Sexual Misconduct

Anybody is more prone to any misconduct if he or she is tired and physically depleted. We have already noted that many pastors are overworked and underpaid. The pastor's poor personal boundaries or the demanding expectations of the congregation may contribute to a workaholic pattern. Such patterns preclude that pastors have the time or willingness to implement adequate physical self-care. Lack of sleep and exercise and a poor diet can be factors that contribute to physical depletion. The stresses of the job and the cultural and theological environment can also take a toll on the body.

We discussed in chapter three the fact that neurochemistry may play a role in patterns of emotional disease and addiction. Neurochemistry can be affected by a variety of environmental factors, including pollution, sunlight, diet, exercise, and rest. Chronic or transient diseases can also affect the chemistry of emotions in the brain creating anger, loneliness, and depression. These feelings can lead to other feelings of entitlement and selfishness, that one needs physical and emotional comfort in some way. Sex can symbolize these kinds of comfort.

We note, finally, that we all need to be touched. Babies who aren't suffer a "failure to thrive" and can even die. Likewise, pastors need to be touched in healthy ways, but their role makes them "untouchable."

It is clear that even the healthiest of individuals can be very vulnerable to unhealthy environment. We move now to consideration of the vulnerability of victims and the factors that contribute toward that condition.

# Chapter Five
# Victims and Vulnerability

Victims are persons who have experienced inappropriate boundary crossing by clergy. To say that a person is a victim is not to describe the degree of culpability of the clergy involved nor make judgments whether or not the victim acted in any inappropriate way. Victims are injured in some way by a professional who, whatever motives may be involved, did not avoid hurting the client. As we proceed with the chapter, the differentials between pastor and parishioner concerning responsibility and power will be clearer.

Victims are vulnerable. When we use the term "vulnerability," we intend to invoke the root meaning of the word (Latin: *vulnus,* wound). *Everyone* has periodic times of "woundability"—a state, a condition, in which being hurt is easier. This again has less to do with degrees of culpability, but everything to do with being subject to injury.

## Sexual Harassment and Vulnerability

Recent awareness of the prevalence of sexual harassment has helped to understand the differences in power between certain roles and how that power can be exploited for intimidation or for sexual access. Sexual harassment has been very prevalent in the church. Linda Majka reported in *Society*[1] that the United Methodist Church surveyed 1578 people in February 1990 and found that 39 percent reported unwanted sexual attention. Fifty percent

[1]May/June 1991, 14–21.

of the clergy responders reported at least one incident. Seventy-seven percent of women clergy reported experiencing harassment. Three percent of the men did so. The most frequent types of problematic behavior were listed in descending order as: (1) unsolicited closeness and touching, (2) unsolicited sexual comments, (3) unsolicited suggestive looks and/or leering, (4) pressure for dates or activities, and (5) promised influence in return for sexual favors.

Sexual harassment or misconduct can range all the way from mild to extremely violent forms. One of the most subtle form of sexual harassment includes creating a "hostile environment," in which acts, words, gestures, attitudes, or objects are used in such a way as to make the victim eventually so uncomfortable that he/she cannot function normally because of internal stress. This is the most subjective and difficult kind of harassment for an investigator to ascertain or adjudicate. If this kind of harassment has occurred, there is usually evidence that the perpetrator continued to act in ways that caused the victim to feel miserable, frightened, cowed, or severely uncomfortable over enough time to cause dysfunctionality in the victim.

Another form of sexual harassment is *quid pro quo* ("this for that") in which someone in power above another person, e.g., a supervisor or teacher or counselor, offers the supervisee, student, or client, some kind of advantage in exchange for sexual favors. "I'll make sure you get your promotion (or grade, or favorable report) if you consent to come over to my house tonight for a special time together." Or, "I'll make sure you're elected to that committee or board if you give me the physical and emotional support I need right now." Although this type of harassment can be quite subtle, most of the time it is not hard to document since it will generally continue and become clearer in intent over a period of time. It is more blatant than the first type.

The third type, sexual violence, occurs when one person takes sexual advantage by sheer force, size, or intimidating threats, culminating in such actions as forcible sexual touching or grabbing not desired by the victim, date rape, or forcible rape. This type is easier to ascertain, except when the complainant has no witnesses or corroborators of any kind, and it is one person's word against another.

Clergy sexual misconduct can include all three of the above types of behaviors. A pastor may make suggestive remarks, or make offers to help the person with personal needs outside the parameters of the immediate counseling issues. In the worst-case scenario the pastor may move forcibly to kiss, fondle, or disrobe the client. Each of these situations describes a different kind or level of vulnerability that is created by the perpetrator or harasser. The response of the victim to the harassing behavior as it develops is also important to maintaining or deepening the level of vulnerability. Persons who are internally strong, self-confident, and secure have more freedom to assertively stand up for themselves and ask the perpetrator to "cease and desist." This may, or may not, have the desired effect.

However, people who are coming to a minister for help are not usually feeling that strong. Sydney Smith describes psychotherapy clients as being in some form of regressed mental state as they come in for help. We should not be surprised, he says, but rather expect, that some clients will not only be capable of falling in love with their therapist, but that some will act or talk in sexually seductive ways due to the confused feelings and uncertain boundaries in their own mind.[2] If a pastoral counselor is not aware of this possibility and ready to deal successfully with it, there is good reason not to allow this person to be involved in long-term counseling. In most cases, only counselors who are being actively monitored by effective supervisors will succeed avoiding problems with vulnerable clients over the long haul.

## General Conditions of Vulnerability

One of the most thorough recent treatments of sexual misconduct by therapists and clergy does not even list supposed vulnerabilities of women clients. Rather the editor chooses to let women tell their stories on their own terms as they experienced them.[3]

[2]Sydney Smith, "The Seduction of the Female Patient," *Sexual Exploitation in Professional Relationship,* ed. Glen Gabbard (Washington, D.C.: American Psychiatric Press, Inc., 1989) 57–60.

[3]Part II, "Victim's Experiences," *Breach of Trust: Sexual Exploitation by Health Care Professionals and Clergy,* ed. John Gonsiorek (Thousand Oaks, Calif.: Sage Publications, 1955) 41–56.

One of those victims tells her story as one in which she goes to a clergyman with several serious previous traumatic experiences:

> From the onset of therapy, my perpetrator convinced me that he would teach me God's love through a fatherly love. He would re-parent me. He told me no one would ever hurt me, not over his dead body. After all, he was a master of therapeutic techniques. I felt as if life's joys and hopes were being presented to me on a silver platter. I was very grateful then for any help in my life, because I was lost and confused.[4]

Thus, when a woman counselee comes in to see a pastor in a state of need, focused upon the problem she wants to solve in counseling, or feeling dependent and somewhat psychologically regressed, she is not as capable of standing up to the pastor's signals of sexual interest in her. Whenever someone asks a professional for help, whether it is an attorney, medical doctor, clergy, professor or psychotherapist, they are coming in the guise of something like the following: "I need help; I feel helpless in some area of my life; I don't feel good about myself; I'm feeling sad, lonely or depressed, and I'm somewhat confused about what to do."

As Marilyn Peterson has so expertly pointed out, when a person in need, male or female, comes to a professional person for help, or leans on a person in authority for safety and support, they are more vulnerable. She describes the position of a needy client as, among other things, one in which the person is dependent, with limited choices, needing to know more, but with a certain loss of freedom to choose because of debilitating anxiety over one's personal problems.[5]

Edelwich and Brodsky put it more succinctly: "The clinician's power is the client's vulnerability."[6] It does not matter what has created the need or what the clinician's actual power is, the very act of asking for help gives power to the clinician.

---

[4] L. Lewis, "Growing Beyond Abuse," ibid., 49.

[5] Marilyn Peterson, *At Personal Risk* (New York: W. W. Norton, 1992) 57. Emphasis ours.

[6] Jerry Edelwich and Archie Brodsky, *Sexual Dilemmas for the Helping Professional* (New York: Brunner/Mazel, 1991) 57.

Other factors make a woman who comes to a spiritual leader for help more vulnerable. Some of these are: seeing the pastor as a father figure, socialization to comply with men in authority, insecurity about personal worth, struggles with her image of God, and seeking out this helper to solve serious unresolved spiritual issues that entangle themselves with her own sense of worth and acceptability before God.[7] Finally, women growing up in families where boundaries are not clearly respected or enforced would experience greater confusion about themselves in relationships with males in general and perhaps even more so in relationships where there is a power differential.

As Richard Sipe has recently pointed out, some church cultures have long shaped our concepts of male-female relationships in terms of males having a denigrated view of women. Women have been portrayed in theological treatises down through the centuries as temptresses, lacking moral discernment, more vulnerable to temptation, in short—a problem for males—sometimes even conceptually allied with the source of all evil, Satan.[8] Whether we are teaching seminarians about personhood, sexuality, or counseling, we must be vigilant as to the kind of effects this kind of teaching has upon both the clergy and their potential victims. It is conceivable that *some* women act in seductive ways because that is what they have been taught is the stance they need to take with males in power over them. This is a broadly systemic kind of issue, and it can only be changed by working with the larger picture, including our biblical hermeneutics and especially our theological anthropology.

## Conditions Specific to Some Clients

Annette Brodsky, chief psychologist and director of training in the department of psychiatry at Harbor-UCLA Medical Center in California, describes the kinds of clients in therapy who might be more vulnerable to therapist misconduct as follows: "The patient

---

[7]George Ohlschlager and Peter Mosgofian, *Law for the Christian Counselor* (Waco, Tex.: Word Publications, 1995) 52.

[8]A. W. Richard Sipe, *Sex, Priests and Power: Anatomy of a Crisis* (New York: Brunner/Mazel, 1995) passim.

is frequently reasonably attractive, young, naïve, dependent, and in need of working on relationships." Brodsky observes them as being especially trusting of their therapists and people who question their own judgment when it conflicts with that of the therapist. She goes on to affirm what we said above about sexual harassment complainants: A patient who commonly becomes sexually involved with his or her therapist is the one who has been physically or sexually abused as a child by his or her own parents. These patients tend to play out the role of abused child with the therapist and become extremely vulnerable to the therapist's demands, however subtle." In addition, vulnerable women patients have "learned to relate to men in authority in ways that are readily sexualized." They may also believe that the therapist is someone who must be obeyed in order to receive care and love. Others are simply inexperienced with males outside their family, and naïvely trusting.[9]

Jerry Edelwich and Archie Brodsky have a section in their volume about therapist sexual misconduct. Psychological or emotional conditions in the client may drive them to use the therapy session in sexualized ways. For example, the client may desire to: (1) gratify sexual desire (when genuinely sexually attracted to the therapist), (2) divert attention from treatment issues, (3) bribe or manipulate, (4) establish an unholy alliance in conjoint therapy, (5) compromise the therapist's position, (6) gain status among one's peers, (7) gain strength through bonding with a stronger person, and (8) gain attention and gratification through the use of accustomed strategies. Edelwich and Brodsky warn that "no therapist should see these goals as particularly personal, since they reflect more than anything else the client's poor learning of coping strategies."[10]

Therefore, the therapist or clergyperson stands responsible to guard the safety of the client and is culpable for not doing so, no matter how the client behaves. Edelwich and Brodsky comment

[9]Carolyn M. Bates and Annette M. Brodsky, *Sex in the Therapy Hour: A Case of Professional Incest* (New York: Guilford, 1989) 137–40. Cf. also Glen Gabbard, *Sexual Exploitation in Professional Relationships* (Washington D.C.: American Psychiatric Press, Inc., 1989) 15–26.

[10]Edelwich and Brodsky, op. cit. (1991) 20–6.

wryly that when a client comes in giving off signals like, "You Tarzan, me Jane," there are too many male counselors who are only too willing to imagine themselves as Tarzan![11]

More commonly, there are people who have experienced emotional neglect by their parents for one reason or another and who now desperately need the approval and affirmation of a parental figure such as a clergyperson. This kind of client calls for some careful counseling under supervision. Even though these cases are not so immediately apparent in terms of level of severity, they present a challenge to a counselor because of high level dependency needs. If such a client is inadvertently matched to a counselor who is desperately lonely and needs to be needed and who lacks guidance or moral scruples with vulnerable people, we have a very explosive situation.

With an increasing population of young people coming out of homes with either divorced parents, blending of families, or being children of chemically dependent parents, there will probably be an exponential increase in the number of counseling clients who have experienced emotional neglect, or abuse, or even emotional trauma. Confused boundaries will be more common for both counselors and counselees. It is important to work with seminarians and clergy in both classroom and continuing education concerning the dangers inherent in these populations.

A rarer but real client condition (about 2 percent of the population, according to the DSM-IV) that creates serious problems for clergy untrained in mental health issues is that of borderline personality disorder. This kind of person has a severe struggle with abandonment issues, unstable self-image or sense of worth. They waiver back and forth between wanting to be close to people and impulsively rejecting them. They will be angry one moment, and dependent the next, or vice versa. In such a condition, a female may use seductive behavior to get close to males, or at the opposite end of the continuum, in anger may seduce in order to hurt or destroy. Clergy facing such people need immediately to seek competent referral and supervision resources in order to stay out of "the danger zone."

[11]Ibid., 8.

There are both personal and socio-cultural reasons why people coming for help are in a vulnerable condition, and that must be vigilantly and respectfully managed by the clergy professional. For clergy counselors and helpers, the more self-awareness, counselor training, supervision, and spiritual discernment, the better. It is time to stop using labels such as "affair" or "other woman" to describe sexual misconduct situations and begin to deal more honestly and frankly with the complexities of interacting with people who come for help who are especially vulnerable. Both an awareness of issues such as transference/countertransference and various conditions of clients will help clergy avoid making damaging mistakes with these vulnerable people.

In this section of the book we have examined the problem of clergy sexual misconduct. Three major factors—clergy dysfunction, victim vulnerability, and environmental factors—converge to create possible moments of sexual offending. In Part Two we present possible solutions. Careful screening and preparation of candidates for ministry can prevent sexual misconduct. We turn now to looking at a description of the elements of a healthy sexuality model that will enable such efforts.

# Part Two
# The Possible Solutions

# Chapter Six

# The Healthy Sexuality Model

In Part One we have attempted to understand the sexually "offending moment," the point at which the unhealthy dynamics of an offender, victim, and the environment converge. In Part Two we will outline ways in which we might begin preventing such moments. In Part One, we talked about the fact that other forms of abuse by a potential sexual offender may precede the sexually offending moment. In Part Two our attention will focus on assessing and developing candidates for ministry in healthy ways. To do this we must begin by understanding what we mean by healthy sexuality. The opposite approach in assessing a person's capacity for destructive sexuality is to assess their capacity for healthy sexuality. The screening of candidates for ministry demands that we have a model of what we mean by healthy sexuality. Our experience in various theological schools and ecclesiastical forums has demonstrated a rather pronounced need for this model. In this chapter we will present a model of healthy sexuality that can be used as a guide to help us in this assessment

We believe that a model of healthy sexuality should be more broadly defined than genital sexuality. It should include wider dimensions of a person's experience than purely biological ones. We also believe that a person's ability to experience healthy sexuality depends on their ability to be close to God, to themselves, and to others. The word intimacy best describes the state of being close. A person can be intimate intellectually, emotionally, spiritually, and/or physically. People can be intimate in one of these areas and not the others. When we broaden the definition in this way, we include the possibility that healthy sexuality may not even involve genital sexuality.

We need to distinguish the difference between the state of intimacy and the capacity to be intimate in healthy ways. The state of intimacy can occur in healthy and unhealthy ways. For example, physical intimacy can occur without emotional, intellectual, or spiritual intimacy being a part of the relationship. From our moral perspective we believe that this is not healthy. The capacity to be intimate includes abilities such as trust, honesty, vulnerability, self-disclosure, response to the other's self-disclosure, courage to take risks, awareness of the needs of the self and of the other, and communication skills.[1]

A healthy person will be able to make healthy choices about which kinds of intimacy are appropriate in a given relationship. They will know and accept the boundaries between the kinds of intimacy. An unhealthy person cannot make these healthy choices because they allow their needs in one area to be confused with their needs in another. For example, a person with deep needs for emotional intimacy may confuse those with needs for physical intimacy. As we have discussed, many who sexually offend are equating sex with love and nurture. Others confuse sex with power and control.

Evaluating and preparing people for ministry, among other things, means that we help them evaluate their capacity for appropriate holistic intimacy. We believe that if a candidate has this capacity, there will be much less likelihood that he or she will sexually offend. This, of course, does not preclude other factors, such as environmental ones, from overcoming even the healthiest of people.

With potential students in the admissions process, there are a few obvious factors that we can pick up through background checks and psychometric evaluation. However, the greater percentage of these students have not as yet acted in ways that cause evaluative or psychometric alarm.

---

[1]For a more complete discussion of the capacity to be intimate, see Lyman C. Wynne and Adele R. Wynne, "The Quest for Intimacy," *Journal of Marital and Family Therapy* (October 1986) 12:4, 383–94.

A model of healthy sexuality should allow us to do two things: First, it should help us identify the capacity for healthy sexuality. Second, it should give us a direction about developing and forming that capacity even in people who in early assessment demonstrate many deficiencies for it. We are not as much interested in screening out as we are in the process of building and forming. In this chapter we would like to outline and explain such a model. In the rest of Part Two, we would like to offer ways of implementing the model.

We also believe that a model of healthy sexuality should not define morality but should fit well with one's own theological and moral interpretations. We propose then that such a model should include the following five interrelated dimensions.[2] These are: (1) personal, (2) relational, (3) behavioral, (4) physical, and (5) spiritual (see *Figure 3*).

*Figure 3:* Healthy Sexuality

Following is an explanation of the key questions and elements of each of these dimensions.

## 1. Personal Dimension

The central questions of this dimension are, "Who am I as a sexual person? What are the messages and identities that I have been given? What impairments did I suffer developmentally that

---

[2][Note: Essential elements adapted with permission from Ginger Manley's article, "Healthy Sexuality: Stage III Recovery" (*The Journal of Sexual Addiction/ Compulsivity* [vol. 2, no. 3, 1995] 157–83). Her article is about treatment of offenders. However, we extrapolate here from her basic model in a positive direction.]

prevent me from being intimate?" The answers to these questions depend on a variety of factors, including:

- *Sexual Identity.* By this we mean whether or not a person considers himself or herself as male or female. In addition, does he or she experience himself or herself as attractive?
- *Sexual Orientation.* What does person consider his or her sexual preference for a sexual partner to be?
- *Sexual Role Assignment.* What messages, cultural and otherwise, has a person received about his or her role as a male or female?
- *Sexual Trauma.* What sexual or other traumas has a person experienced that will affect his or her perception of self as a sexual being and his or her ability to function as a sexual partner?
- *Developmental History.* How has a person completed the developmental stages appropriate to their age? How does this affect the person's ability to attach and bond in healthy ways?

When we discover dysfunction in any of these areas it is an obvious danger signal. Such dysfunction may or may not reflect serious psychological pathology as might be diagnosed on Axis II of DSM-IV Remember that the results of the Irons/Laaser study of twenty-five offenders revealed almost no serious Axis II personality disorders. Such dysfunction, however, does reflect a serious vulnerability to the influence of other dysfunctional factors.[3]

One of the most obvious dysfunctions would be that of unresolved sexual trauma. The shame, anger, and fear of this condition predisposes a person to be vulnerable to unhealthy sexual expression. Sexual trauma experienced at crucial developmental phases may also impair a person's ability to bond or have healthy relationships. For example, a man traumatized in early development may have anger at the gender of the perpetrator or at the gender of the parent or guardian who neglected to protect him from the trauma. How will this anger be played out?

---

[3] *The Diagnostic and Statistical Manual of Mental Disorder* (Washington, D.C.: American Psychiatric Association, 1994, 5th ed.) 424–9.

Such questions cause us to wonder about appropriateness for ministry of sexual-trauma victims. Is a sexual trauma victim who has not involved themselves in a healing process ready to enter ministry and be vulnerable to the projection of previous injuries onto others who are under his or her care?

## 2. The Relational Dimension

The basic question of this dimension is: "Who am I in relation to others?"

We believe that relationships are experienced at three levels:

a) *Primary Relations.* This is a relationship with a significant or committed other such as a mate, spouse, or partner. This may or may not include genital/sexual expression. For example, an engaged couple are "significant" and "committed" to each other but may choose, because of theological convictions, not to engage in genital sexual expression until marriage.

b) *Secondary Relations.* These may be enduring and committed relationships and can include touch or physical contact (e.g., hugs), emotional vulnerability, and communication, but not genital sex. Friends, colleagues, primary and extended family members, church members, and members of any other meaningful communities (fraternal organizations, clubs, athletic teams, twelve-step groups, therapy groups, etc.).

c) *Tertiary Relations.* These are distant or temporary relationships and attachments. These relationships may experience honesty, vulnerability, communication, touch and risk taking but do not involve long term association and commitment. Sometimes it is easier to be open and honest with such relations because we know that we will not see these people again nor can they use information about us against us.

These three levels describe relationships that are mutual. They will involve give and take. Relationships between clergy and parishioners may involve elements of category b and c, but are not mutual. Clergy are care givers by definition of their role. Parishioners are care receivers. Clergy and parishioner roles are by definition not mutual. The concept of transference should inform clergy that a parishioner may be assigning power to the clergy role even if the clergy person, at a personal level, does not feel empowered.

When we were both student chaplains at the University of Iowa Hospital, one of us was assigned to the Coronary Care Unit. Regular visits were made for several days to an elderly Jewish woman. The visits were friendly and not particularly "religious." An assumption was being made by us that these visits were more mutual because of the difference in religious background. A part of us liked them being mutual out of our own insecurity and loneliness. At the end of her time this woman said to us, "Thank you, Rabbi." To which we replied, "I'm not a rabbi." The woman emphatically said, "You've been a rabbi to me!"

Examples like this illustrate that a parishioner, or a person assigned to our care, may have very different perceptions of the relationship than we do. It is important that we continually seek to articulate these perceptions of relationship. When such articulation is not possible, we should always assume that the relationship is not mutual and that clergy role is being empowered.

We must also remember that there will also be times when a parishioner consciously says that they would like the clergy relationship to be more mutual but unconsciously feels differently. The unconscious transference by the parishioner still gives the clergy definite power.

Our work in Part One demonstrates that clergy may often long for the parishioner relationship to be more mutual. The clergy role is often isolating and lonely. Unconscious wounds may make clergy extremely vulnerable to their own relational needs. When emotional and sexual needs are felt, as we know, this is a very dangerous situation.

It is always safer to assume an imbalance in power and mutuality between clergy and parishioner. This is a healthy boundary to maintain as lonely as it may be for clergy. Due to the constantly shifting nature of the relationships between people in ministry and the people they live and work with, guarding this boundary is often difficult. One moment clergy are working like peers on a committee; the next, they are playing volleyball together in the church gym; later, they may visit one of them at their hospital bedside. Then, clergy see them in their office to deal with personal crises. Just as a child marvels at the ever-shifting arrangements in a kaleidoscope, so those in ministry often wonder just what their role with a particular church member might be at a given moment. Are they committee colleagues, fellow members of the faith community, prayer partners, volleyball team mates, or counselors?

In recent efforts to empower the laity, this issue occurs even more frequently. There is a sense in which clergy are being asked to become more collegial than ever and to share more authority and leadership influence with lay people. This calls for a constant alertness to how the roles and boundaries are to be safeguarded. People in ministry need to be constantly aware of the ways that the settings they work in shift and how those shifts affect boundaries and roles. The person in ministry must be responsible at all times to monitor and safeguard those boundaries of people under their care, whatever the setting.

Our model of healthy sexuality assumes that a person must maintain healthy relationships at all three levels—primary, secondary, and tertiary. Some of us in recovery from sexual offending or addiction have found that maintaining healthy relationships at all levels helps to mitigate unhealthy sexual expression. One cannot expect his or her primary relationship to meet all emotional and spiritual needs. When there is this expectation, there is often great tension. For example, a person cannot expect a yes or no answer from a sexual partner to symbolize all acceptance and relational needs.

If this assumption is true, it is imperative that clergy maintain healthy relationships at the primary, secondary, and tertiary level that are not subject to the authority of their role. These are mutual relationships: spouses, partners, colleagues, and friends outside the immediate community of faith. One of the questions that is inherent here is: "Where do clergy find their own community of faith of which they are not the leader?"

Candidates for ministry should be able to demonstrate an ability to form and maintain such relationships as a prerequisite to ordination.

### 3. *The Behavioral Dimension*

The two basic question of this dimension are: "Am I able to exercise positive choice in my sexual activities?" "Am I able to be emotionally and spiritually intimate with a partner in appropriate ways or do I participate in other behaviors that allow me to escape my feelings."

It is helpful to look at this dimension in terms of extremes. Pat Carnes first described a polarity in unhealthy sexual expression very similar to that found in eating disordered people. Diagrammed it looks like this:

| Under Eating | Normal Eating | Over Eating |
|---|---|---|
| Anorexia | | Bulimia |
| AVOIDANCE | HEALTHY SEXUALITY | OVERINDULGENCE |
| "Acting In" | | "Acting Out" |
| Aversive | | Immersive |

*Figure 4*

Sexually, there are those who exhibit unmanageable avoidance behaviors. They virtually turn off their sexuality. They are sexually "anorexic." They may avoid others, be aversive to contact, and use rigid and tight controls to stop being sexual. This rigidity has been referred to as "Acting In." For some, consciously and unconsciously, this lack of sexual expression may be an attempt to control painful memories of sexual trauma and experience. For others, it may be an attempt to control the despair of future acting out.

Sexual "Over Eaters" overindulge in sex. This pattern has been called sexual addiction by Carnes and others because it reflects several key features. It is repetitive, degenerative, and destructive. It becomes unmanageable. Sexual addicts may also be trying to control and medicate (mood alter) early memories of trauma, feelings of despair, and/or a sense of abandonment and loneliness. Sexual "bulimia" may also reflect an addictive pattern. It differs in that a person will do something to themselves to self-punish and purge the experience. One of us worked with a man who plucked out both of his eyes (a biblical injunction in Matthew 5:29) because of an uncontrollable pornography addiction.

Screening candidates for ministry for one of these two unhealthy patterns will involve a detailed sexual history. Carnes, for example, has published two instruments that can be helpful in such a history. The Sexual Addiction Screening Test is a shorter, true/false questionnaire that can be used to assess the presence of sexual addiction. The Sexual Dependency Inventory can be used to aid in diagnosis but assumes the strong possibility of sexual addiction. In this assumption it provides detailed information on the nature of the problem and also investigates etiologic factors. The validity of both such instruments depends on a candidate's ability to be honest.[4]

We believe that candidates for ministry should be able to demonstrate freedom from any sexually dysfunctional pattern, addiction or not. In the presence of dysfunction or addiction, a process of healing and/or "sobriety" must be a part of the formation process.

In addition to a sexual history, the behavioral dimension also asks if a candidate is practicing any other behavior that would prevent him/her from being present and vulnerable to their emotions and available to relationships. Alcoholism, for example, would be such a behavior. Any other addictive or avoidance pattern should be diagnosed. Just as with sexually dysfunctional behavior, a candidate must be able to engage in and maintain a process of healing and/or sobriety.

The behavioral dimension assumes that those who suffer from addiction may be using the addictive substance or behavior as a substitute for intimacy. Food addicts, for example, may use food in general or a particular food when they are lonely. Similarly, sex addicts use sexual experience and real or imagined sexual partners as a substitute for real closeness. Particularly those who use sex as a substitute for love will be vulnerable to sexual misconduct in ministry.

One of the important clinical factors in the behavioral dimension is to assess whether or not a candidate experiences a dissociative process. Trauma survivors may experience, for example, Post Traumatic Stress Disorder (PSTD). This is a condition in which a person literally "leaves" or dissociates from their painful emotions when they are triggered by painful memories.

[4]Patrick Carnes, *Don't Call It Love: Recovery from Sexual Addiction* (New York: Bantam Books, 1991) appendix A, 394–413.

Those in recovery from addiction, trauma, PSTD, and other dysfunctional patterns can be wonderfully effective pastors. They demonstrate a humility and capacity for empathy because of their own accepted brokenness, and that can be a wonderful gift.

### 4. The Physical Dimension

The basic questions of this dimension are: "Is my body responding physically to its full sexual capacity? Do I understand, like, respect, and nurture my body?"

Intimacy with one's body demands that one knows it and understands how it functions and dysfunctions. Even in our enlightened time as heir to the pioneering work of the last several decades, many are totally ignorant of the human sexual response and sexual anatomy. This may be particularly true if there is sexual dysfunction present. Acquiring such knowledge and/or therapeutic intervention is part of the work of this dimension.

Being comfortable with one's body is also part of intimacy in the physical dimension. Historical experience of sexual shame may prevent a person from this level of comfort. This would certainly be true of sexual-trauma survivors. It can also be true of those who have been sexually teased or made fun of based on some physical characteristic. Then, too, are those who grow up in silence about sexuality and physical bodies. They are left feeling like sexual outcasts for what may even be normal sexual feelings. If people do not feel comfortable with their own bodies, no other person can really convince them that they are attractive.

Being intimate with one's body means that one is able to nurture it in healthy ways. Eating right, exercising, seeking appropriate medical care, getting enough rest, and wearing comfortable and attractive clothes may be indicators of this kind of physical intimacy. Medical assessment can be a part of the screening process of this dimension. Where there is a sexual dysfunction, medical intervention and therapy will be necessary.

All of the dimensions overlap. Here we see how medical and psychological assessment must cooperate. If a man experiences impotence, for example, there can be emotional or physical etiologies present. Obese persons, similarly, may experience medical, genetic, or psychological reasons for a pattern of overeating.

## 5. The Spiritual Dimension

The basic question of this dimension is, "Am I centered and connected with God? Do I feel validated as a sexual human being, and can I experience meaningfulness in my relationships, behave in congruence with my values, and express my physical/sexual functions as my God intends?" Do I reverence and respect the guidelines of Scripture for my sexuality? Am I willing to live according to those guidelines?

Candidates for ministry should be encouraged to have spiritual intimacy with God as they understand God, and with each other. Various denominations will differently interpret how spiritual intimacy should be formed. However, we recommend avoiding extremes such as spiritualizing all problems, on the one hand, or, on the other, ignoring the power of the spiritual life and assessing it simply as a psychological function.

Some attempt should be made to assess the nature of spiritual intimacy that a candidate experiences. Is it true connection with God, or is it performance of learned practices? It is easy, for some, to learn the ways and practices of a certain religious community or faith tradition. Does such a candidate mimic common practice in order to fit in, or does he or she sincerely feel the transcendent connection?

We have known many candidates, for example, who rigorously perform spiritual practices. They pray, read Scripture, and attend religious services. They do not experience, however, spiritual intimacy or peace nor freedom from any dysfunctional behaviors. Martin Luther is an example of someone who as a seminarian could not pacify his spiritual anxiety.[5]

If the spiritual life is pursued in isolation without community, there is also a danger of losing touch with reality. We have known some, for example, whose religious life was experienced in such isolation that they were capable of compartmentalizing their mental life, especially their fantasies, from it.

The spiritual identity of a healthy candidate for ministry will have a sense of true calling. It is dangerous to try to evaluate such subjective experience for someone else. An attempt should

---

[5]Erik Erikson, *Young Man Luther* (New York: W. W. Norton, 1958, 1962).

be made, however, to determine if a candidate is trying to please someone else, inner voices from the past, or a true sense of calling from God. A friend of ours, for example, threatens to write a paper entitled "Being Ordained by Your Mother and Not by the Church."

True calling also suggests that a candidate is not trying to heal old wounds or find approval in the role of ministry. In an earlier paper we referred to this as "Ordination as a shame reduction strategy." It is the hope that one will be transformed into a new being, free of shame, and full of external approval. One female pastor who has offended against men in her church referred to this hope as the "Wish for Ontological Transformation."

Finally, the spiritual dimension suggests that a person be able to live in a way that is consistent with his or her sexual values. Do they have a history of violating their own sense of morals? If they have done so even in minor ways historically, they are vulnerable to doing so in major ways in the future. Sexual offending is full of delusions, denial, and rationalizations. None of the offending pastors that we have known have been fully sociopathic personalities. At some point they had to talk themselves into crossing their own moral boundaries.

Perhaps one of the areas of investigation that is important is how candidates understand the integration of their sexuality with their spirituality. What role do their faith and beliefs play in dealing with sexual relationships? Do they respect the bodies and the boundaries of others? Do they humbly and repentantly accept grace for any past sexual sins, or do they rationalize their sins?

All of the dimensions of the healthy sexuality model are interrelated. They affect each other and can really only be isolated for the reason of academic clarity. The integration of the dimensions is most clear when we see how dysfunction in one dimension affects the other four. For example, if a person has not resolved sexual trauma issues, it will affect all of the other dimensions in some ways. Relationally, the person will be withdrawn and unable to disclose important parts of his or her past; behaviorally, various addictive, compulsive, or dysfunctional escapes will be used to avoid feelings; physically, the genital sexual relationship will be impaired and physical self-care compromised, not to mention various psychosomatic complaints that are possible; spiritually, a person's ability to trust has been impaired particularly in those cases in which the perpetrator is a religious authority.

More positively, if a person is healthy in one dimension, there can be a positive impact on the other four areas. Relationally, intimacy with one's spouse and others makes it less likely that a person will look for substitutes for intimacy behaviorally. It also mitigates against anger and loneliness and the possibility of exploiting others for personal gain. The understanding of one's roles at various social and professional levels and how these roles affect others is a form of healthy relational empathy that can prevent abuse of power and role. Physically, if one can respect and nurture one's own body, one will be better able to respect another's and maintain healthy boundaries. Spiritually, intimacy makes it more likely that a person will know the true intentions of one's heart and would be more likely to act in congruence with one's morals.

## Outcomes

A healthy candidate for ministry will be working on all dimensions of the healthy sexuality model at the same time. This can be very challenging. In summary, candidates will demonstrate the following qualities:

1. Be comfortable with their own sexual identity and sexual preference.
2. Be in a healing process for any early life trauma.
3. Demonstrate the capacity to be intimate and have healthy attachments and bonds.
4. Understand the difference between different levels of intimacy and the appropriate boundaries between them.
5. Understand the power of the ministerial role and the dynamics of transference and countertransference.
6. Maintain healthy primary and secondary relationships including marriage and friendships.
7. Maintain sobriety from any addictive or unhealthy behaviors.
8. Demonstrate a healthy ability to be in touch with and express feelings.

9. Maintain appropriate physical self-care.
10. Work through the various reasons for a call to ministry, examining their motives and expectations.
11. Demonstrate a healthy private and communal spiritual life.

It has been our intention in this chapter to describe an emotionally healthy person so that candidates for ministry can be assisted in comparing the sexuality they perceive in their own internal framework with this model in order to be able to make corrections and predictions about their own attitudes and conduct. Now we move to the educational efforts seminaries and ecclesiastical bodies can make in order to help candidates deal with the cognitive, spiritual, contextual, and social aspects of their sexuality.

# Chapter Seven
# Cognitive Education

We have observed that when students are presented with helpful information about the various areas discussed in this book, they often want to know more. That is encouraging, but students need to give attention to the entire spectrum of their personal and developmental issues. Cognitive education is done not only in the classroom but also in small groups, personal reflection, field education, and social relationships.

There are helpful topics that can be incorporated into courses in a seminary curriculum that would encourage students to process their struggles with their own sexuality. We are not necessarily suggesting that seminaries produce brand new courses. We are well aware that faculty people are resistant to adding new courses since to do so often means encroaching upon someone's disciplinary territory. Most faculty will protest that they cannot get through all the "expected material" as it is. We might begin, therefore, by helping faculty from the various disciplines to consider ways to bring up and process this topic within already established courses. However, if we grasp the issue as an important enough topic for us all to work with from whatever academic perspective we employ, there is hope that students will hear what they need to hear from us. The broader the spectrum of persons they hear from, the better for their learning.

If, for example, we were to list certain theological, ethical, and biblical topics that relate to the issue of sexuality and ministry and ask professors to deal more thoroughly with them, this might have some benefits, depending on the professors and their interests, openness, and capacity to work with the topics raised.

Professors in each discipline will need to examine the following list and ask whether or where they might insert ideas, concepts, or units, or simply opportunities for students to explore them in class assignments.

## Biblical/Theological Areas

Biblical/theological topics of relevance to sexuality would include such topics as the relationship of sexuality to the *imago Dei;* theology of marriage, including divorce, women, sexuality, singleness, and family; personal and corporate sanctification of sexuality; community sexual ethics; a theology of disability, including mental and physical illness; the compulsive/addictive disorders; theological underpinnings for church discipline, for structures and policies for sexual misconduct.

## Sexuality

We would like to make a case for team teaching of such courses, so that a holistic and multidisciplinary approach to the issues might be encouraged. For example, a theologian-ethicist, a biblical scholar, and a specialist in ministry formation could well collaborate on such a course. In schools where spiritual direction is employed, a course offering might well include a spiritual mentor or director to teach students how to integrate their spirituality and sexuality. Gender balance of such staffing is also desirable.

A separate course in human sexuality might include many of the above biblical/theological topics in a seminary setting, depending upon the theological skills of the professor. Generally, such a course might tend to focus more on the social, psychological, and physical aspects of sexuality, but skilled intentionality could remedy this tendency.

Beyond the standard lists of desired topics for sexual education, the theological professor would want to include a generous portion of material on sexual ethics, biblical anthropology, and guidelines for decision-making processes, both for personal growth and for counseling settings. We would recommend strongly that such a course include a strong unit on family systems, with focus on the issues of healthy versus unhealthy influences made by families of origin upon individual emotional and sexual development. The material in chapter six points in that direction.

Biblical stories and pericopes could be used as discussion points for students' processing. For example: the creation story in Genesis 1; the story of Noah's nakedness in Genesis 9; the story of Lot in Genesis 19; Samson, Judges 13ff.; the Levite and his concubine in Judges 19; David and Bathsheba, 2 Samuel 11–12; Amnon and Tamar in 2 Samuel 13; the Song of Songs; Hosea; passages from the Sermon on the Mount, Matthew 5:27-30 and 5:31-32; Matthew 19:3-12 (and parallels); the woman caught in adultery, John 8:1-11; various passages in the epistles about spiritual leaders, relationships between women and men, sexual purity, marriage, and divorce. For example, to cite only a few: 1 Corinthians 7; Romans 13:13-14; Galatians 5:16-26; Ephesians 4:19-20; 5:5, 18; Colossians 3:5-6; 1 Thessalonians 4:3-8; Jude 4, 7-8, 18-19; 2 Peter 2. These passages would all need to be interpreted carefully in context, drawing out the generally applicable theological principles of healthy and Christian views of sexuality for our day and with a biblically-guided balance between the positives and the negatives concerning sexuality.

## Pastoral Care and Counseling

It could be argued that if there is a natural spot for material on sexuality, it would be in pastoral care and counseling.[1] To her surprise, doctoral researcher Sally Conklin found through her recent questionnaire returned from twenty five seminaries in the United States that teaching of human sexuality courses was done by people from all over the disciplinary map. Certainly, most pastoral care and counseling professors would likely have more exposure to the topic and its areas of concern, but because of the personal-interest factor, people from biblical studies or theology

---

[1]Sarah C. "Sally" Conklin, "Sexuality Education of Clergy in Seminaries and Theological Schools," Ph.D. dissertation for the University of Pennsylvania Graduate School of Education, 1996. Summary available from The Center for Sexuality and Religion, P.O. Box 945, South Orange, NJ 07079-0945.

seem to be just as active teaching in this area as are pastoral care people.

Ms. Conklin defines sexuality education in theological schools as needing the following elements:

> (1) balance in sexuality teaching between emphasizing sexual health/vitality and sexual harm/abuse; (2) integrating concepts and methods such as (a) spirituality and sexuality, (b) sexual health and justice, particularly regarding sexual orientation, (c) thinking and feeling in educating for wholeness with compassion, and (d) multidisciplinary approaches, recognizing the pertinence of sexuality for all theological study [we would add: there is also pertinence of theological study for sexuality].[2]

Beyond the usual teachings in pastoral care and counseling courses about transference and countertransference in counseling, however, it would be important to introduce students to the whole spectrum of ethical issues for people helping. Supervision of a student's counseling would provide an important opportunity to help the individual examine their sexual concerns as they reflect upon the counseling process. In courses on marriage and family counseling sexuality could be elaborated quite significantly. While students are studying others' problems in this area, they can think about their own concerns and implications for work in ministry.

## Seminary Examples

One seminary includes a unit of sexuality in ministry in the "Formation for Ministry" course, a first-year orientation to preparation for ministry. The topic is approached by describing issues such as clergy sexual misconduct, sexual harassment, special factors in ministry that create opportunity or vulnerability, family of origin sources of misconduct, accountability resources and frameworks, and questions and answers in break-out sessions for singles and marrieds. The basic pastoral care course also includes a unit on sexual "red flags" for counseling and ministry.

Another seminary has a longer team-taught course on sexuality in ministry in which students read novels that portray the

[2]Ibid.

struggle and temptations people in ministry have with their sexuality. Reading and discussing novels helps students hold the issue a little more at arm's length and is less intimidating for them. Journaling and process are important elements of the course. They hold small group discussion of their readings, including personal sharing of their own views on the issues. Lectures touch on family-of-origin issues, etiology of clergy sexual misconduct, and theological issues related to the topic.

A third seminary also uses team-teaching with a priest and a psychologist collaborating and interacting with students on issues such as celibacy, its history and development, personal processing of one's calling and vocation to celibate ministry, and work areas for integration of one's sexuality and spiritual growth.

## Sexual-Integration Outcomes

It would be imperative that each school and church denomination put some energetic thought into formulating desired cognitive outcomes. The question throughout is: "Is this person ready to deal with: (1) their personal influence as pertains to sexual feelings; (2) the context of ministry in such a way as to model healthy relationship strengths, and (3) a need for humility concerning their weaknesses?" Cognitive outcomes need describing in order to understand the appropriate parameters of cognition in our candidates for ministry. See the outcomes appendix for the complete outcomes' list.

The candidate will be able to demonstrate the following cognitive outcomes:

1. The theological and biblical elements of a Christian view of sexuality.
2. The interrelationship of the various systems a candidate is a member of.
3. Human sexuality and its relationship to personality, dating, marriage and family.
4. Gender issues.
5. Sexual ethics.
6. Relevant counseling ethics, including understanding transference, countertransference, and projection.

7. Guidelines for self-care and other-care; how to build and maintain maximal sexual health and respect for self and others.
8. How to avoid invasion of sexual and other boundaries and understand what constitutes abuse.
9. The legal, financial, psychological, familial, spiritual, and ecclesiastical consequences of sexual misconduct by persons in ministry; will know consequences as described from the standpoint of primary and secondary victims or by perpetrators themselves.

We now move ahead to a description of the spiritual elements of personal formation in order to integrate into candidates' awareness the role of spirituality in sexual feelings, attitudes, and actions.

# Chapter Eight

# Spiritual Formation and Sexuality

## Introduction

In our survey of ATS Seminaries in 1994, we included a question about integration of spiritual life with sexual conduct. For many respondents, this drew a blank. Several respondents wrote on their questionnaire: "I don't understand the question." What does this comment tell us? They are probably aware that somehow spiritual life involves sexuality, but they may lack awareness of a model of a truly integrated approach for it whether for themselves or for teaching students.

One important issue flagged here is that we are challenged to move people in theological schools from a more cognitive conception of their spirituality to one that touches every aspect of their being. Education and spirituality that change lives must touch the core of the self and every one of its ways of relating to the world around us.

## The Shaping of Inner Attitudes

Let me illustrate from another area of life. From eight years living in a Latin American country, I (N.F.) can testify that there is something different about the internal reference-points and values of Latin Americans concerning stop signs and other traffic rules. A four-way stop intersection simply will not work in most of Latin America. To a North American observer, Latins appear to believe it is every individual's unique right to be the first one through the intersection! Numerous times Latin Americans who have visited in the United States and Canada have told me that they cannot believe how orderly and law-abiding North American motorists are. It is possible to discern cultural shaping concerning the way we come to believe and abide by certain traffic guidelines.

The same issue can be identified in terms of observing interpersonal boundaries. We learn to observe and respect each other's boundaries in a particular context that sets up expectations and attitudinal ideals. To our detriment, too often we have come at this topic from the standpoint of being concerned most with putting up stop signs and catching law breakers instead of educating motorists so that they desire, and invest themselves in, safety for all. Added to this concern is our consciousness that simply educating someone cognitively is not going to be sufficient for real change. Ethical standards only help us to a point. All kinds of issues are involved here, including how we internalize values, how we learn to exercise true *agape*-love that is truly disinterested and unselfish. How can we evaluate whether someone really possesses such an inner orientation? How can we change that orientation if it is operating wrongly? This constitutes a real challenge!

An illustration of this need is to think about how to develop a deep respect for people of the opposite sex, their individual boundaries, and personhood. We lament the fact that people coming into seminaries lack this kind of training, but it appears that it is needed. If not, why are so many people having trouble with respecting boundaries? With the breakdown of moral standards and the exponential increase in blending of families, it is no surprise that many of our young people come to the seminary confused about how to observe interpersonal boundaries of all kinds since they have experienced so many shifts and contradictions around them.

These issues must be addressed by our seminaries and churches so that every individual may form an attitudinal direction that will be confirmed by the whole group. This affirmation will be based on deeply held beliefs and values that are consonant with our spiritual and theological commitments. At this point in this book, we address the spiritual formation sector of this issue in the life of the person preparing for ministry.

## Spirituality

"Spirituality" is one of those difficult words to define in such a way as to have concrete usefulness. We found a helpful way in an older Association of Theological Schools' document, where Tilden Edwards defines spirituality as "that most subtle, integral dimension of our awareness, where we sense and trust ourselves belonging through and beyond our ego image to a larger, invaluable horizon that impinges on all we are and do." The question that remains is: Does this definition of spirituality include and incorporate our sexuality, and once it does, is that spirituality a dominating force in determining how we exercise our sexual values and actions?[1]

To help us toward our goal we need to return here to the five-point model of Ginger Manley that we presented in chapter six. The spiritual arena of our sexuality constitutes a vital integrating element of the whole. To neglect or underestimate its essential role is to endanger the well-being of the whole.

Ginger Manley also states:

> Spiritual sexuality involves the very core of one's being—the spark that gives us energy, the backbone that supports us, and the connection that sustains and nurtures us. Spirituality and sexuality are connected at a very basic level in terms of value and meaningfulness about any of the peripheral dimensions, the position of love in one's life, the miracle of existence, and the development and affirmation of sexual grace.[2]

Though there are many approaches to spiritual formation taken by seminaries and church bodies, we will here point out some critical areas for each to consider in their particular seminary setting with an eye to integration of sexuality with spirituality and the prevention of compartmentalization.

[1]Tilden H. Edwards, Jr., director, ATS-Shalem Institute on Spirituality, Washington, D.C., "Spiritual Formation in Theological Schools: Ferment and Challenge," *Theological Education* (Autumn 1980) 7–52. Cf. also the report of the task force on spiritual development in *Theological Education* (Spring 1972).
[2]Ginger Manley, *American Journal of Preventive Psychiatry* (Spring 1991) 3:1, 34.

In some people, there is high dependence upon performing the right spiritual behaviors and not enough consideration of how balanced internal/external wholeness is achieved. The messages some theological students get may be that their spiritual life is their own business, meaning it does not have much consequence on practical issues, or to be considered mostly on an intellectual/cognitive level, with little assistance at integration with their sexuality. However, there are ways to help students to bridge those gaps.

## Background Issues

In almost every ecclesiastical and theological tradition, we observe pendulum swings between an emphasis upon cognitive understanding of faith and a focus upon "heart-religion." Whole movements have grown up in reaction to this tendency to "hyper-intellectualize" the faith. For example, the historically influential *Rule of St. Benedict* of the Benedictine Order and several other monastic movements have focused on the need for balance of heart and head, work and prayer. In seventeenth-century Pietism and its call to genuine personal experience with God, we observe a reaction to scholastic Lutheran hyper-orthodoxy that was failing to meet the deep personal needs of people who had just gone through the horrors of the Thirty-Year War. Philipp Jakob Spener and August Franke called people to a deeply personal faith and a wholesome commitment to obedience that integrated the emotions and will with the intellect. In Europe, the early Moravian movement with its call to whole-hearted commitment strongly influenced John Wesley and the launching of Methodism. American revival movements such as The Great Awakening and the anti-Calvinist movement of Charles Finney called people to new levels of "heart religion." These examples remind us that spiritual formation must look seriously at helping people preparing for ministry to integrate all the areas of the self, cognitive, conative, emotive, and attitudinal.

As Wayne Fehr and Donald Hands put it after treating hundreds of clergy sexual offenders: "We find that clergy who manifest sexual misconduct or transgress boundaries generally are impoverished as far as intimacy with self, others, and God is concerned." Their thesis is that genuine integration honestly faces and addresses sexuality in the total context of intimacy with self, others, and God.[3] We could not agree more.

Hands and Fehr develop a model that posits the possibility of grounding ourselves daily in a posture of silent adoration of God, to let ourselves be loved and affirmed at the deepest level. Their summary of this position is as follows: "Corresponding to the trinitarian mystery of Father, Son, and Spirit, one can let oneself be *creature* (not self-creating or self-validating), *forgiven and beloved sinner* (not self-righteous), and known, forgiven, and loved by others as a *member of the one Body* (not self-sufficient)."[4]

Young people are hungering for reality in this regard. We observe, for example, the great responsiveness by college students to writers and speakers on the Christian college circuit such as Brennon Manning, with his call to thoroughly integrate what typically has been a Roman Catholic emphasis upon love for God with a Protestant emphasis upon trust in God.[5] He calls upon his readers to let go of our inner "Impostor," whose ruse is to get us to hide behind our performance, and to embrace in love and faith the God who is completely for us in Christ and the Cross.

Roman Catholics and Protestants are learning from each other in regard to integration of spirituality to life. Loyola professor Robert J. Wicks' *Handbook of Spirituality for Ministers,* though representing mostly the Roman Catholic tradition, is being widely read by Protestants.[6] Unfortunately, there are not more than a couple of passing references to sexuality in the book. There remains a paucity of written materials to aid the integration of spirituality with sexuality.

In our survey of theological seminaries we discovered that two Roman Catholic schools particularly stand out in the thoroughness with which they work on integration: Kendrick School of Theology (St. Louis, Missouri) and St. John's School of Theology (Collegeville, Minnesota). Kendrick's dean co-teaches (with

---

[3]Wayne Fehr and Donald Hands, *Spiritual Wholeness for Clergy* (Washington, D.C.: The Alban Institute, 1993) 43, 45.

[4]Ibid., 63.

[5]Brennon Manning, *Abba's Child: The Cry of the Heart for Intimate Belonging* (Colorado Springs, Colo.: NavPress, 1994).

[6]Robert J. Wicks, *Handbook of Spirituality for Ministers* (New York: Paulist Press, 1994).

a woman therapist) a course on celibacy that includes both theological and psychological assistance for students in consideration of the issues of their sexuality. St. John's also has a male-female duo teaching their intensive workshop on sexuality and spirituality, with readings from current literature that illustrate in lectures and discussion groups the struggles of people in ministry with sexual issues.

On the Protestant-Evangelical side we found ample descriptions of spiritual formation and specialized faculty, and pertinent courses in the catalogs of Fuller Seminary (Pasadena, California), Asbury Seminary (Wilmore, Kentucky), and Western Seminary (Portland, Oregon). The question still remains as to whether these efforts will lead students to an integration with their sexual development and consciousness.[7]

## Integration Blocks

There are major blocks to integration. We have the usual internal blocks such as toxic shame and shame-based family background, family systems where secret-keeping is dominant, and lacking in live, attractive, and accessible human models. Aligned with this, there are also significant difficulties with discussing personal issues in places that are not safe to expose vulnerable topics. In fact, many students would find seminaries to be inhospitable environments for processing personal issues while working toward ordination. Students encounter few structured opportunities to work on sexuality face-to-face with good models who integrate well their own sexuality and spirituality in their own lives. Too often there is an underdeveloped seminary community life in regard to these issues.

To overcome these blocks we need to consider carefully how to provide students with opportunities where they not only can safely accomplish these tasks but also set expectations and clearly defined objectives/outcomes for an integrative process. We need to make the student responsible to follow up on these objectives, and we should invite them to do so without threat or penalty for "being in process."

---

[7]This information was gathered from recently published catalogs of each of these schools.

We also need to work with faculty in order to empower them to appropriately share their own struggles with integration as part of their teaching and mentoring; e.g., how certain biblical passages and theological concepts apply to the development of spiritual vitality and maturity, especially in regard to putting our sexuality in a context that will be spiritually cohesive and integral with our theological values.

We need to help students obtain guidance/counseling for family of origin issues that are relevant to toxic shame, sexual trauma, and addiction issues. We can also provide safe group processes appropriate for this integration topic.

Spiritual mentors should be educated and alert to the ways an integration issue arises, and how to follow through with clues to problematic sexual struggles. Our theological and ethics courses can provide important descriptions of relationships and distinctions between social and genital intimacy—ways "love hunger" is related both to spiritual life and social networks. Courses in spirituality ought to contain units on integration with sexuality, and vice versa.

Above all, we can work at motivating students to seek all the resources they need to develop and maintain a healthy and balanced life, with their spirituality at the core of that development. We can help students examine their understanding of vital, passionate connectedness to their faith and spiritual resources to the rest of their lives. We can raise before them a model of integration that has a positive tenor of excitement in being invited by God to follow hard after joyful communion with God, while keeping a humble awareness of their own need for disciplined humility and awareness of needs that are to be met appropriately.

John Keller, a well-known author on the spirituality of recovery from alcoholism, tells us that recovery is more than just not drinking; it is learning, living, and reinforcing a whole new way of life. Ultimately spirituality in recovery is learning, living, and reinforcing a new way of life in which each day there is recognition and acceptance of personal limitation, of being met by God and others in that limitation, and of moving toward growth within that limitation with hope and meaning.[8]

[8]John Keller, "Spirituality in Recovery," unpublished paper, 22.

Theological input is needed to help students consider the dangers of viewpoints that degrade or objectify people of either sex in such a way as to lose respect or ability to observe boundaries and to value each other in true *agape*-love. This is one of the major points made by Richard Sipe, who makes a well-documented but decidedly controversial case that a prevalent theological-cultural view of women lies behind some of the misconduct by clergy.[9]

Ethics classes ought to work intensely with how our faith convictions get moved from the cognitive area to a passionate devotion to act in conformity to God's will. We must integrate our convictions into daily choices that have to do with treating other people with the highest respect and observation of their value in God's eyes and the ways God calls every person we meet or know into a higher relationship with God's will and the Body of Christ.

### The New Person in Christ

We seminary professors need to look at how the sanctification of a Christian leader happens. Formation in seminary life involves creating a new awareness of personal responsibility before one's ability to change toward the "new creation" in Christ.[10] Spiritual formation and direction deal with helping people examine their consciousness of the role of the Holy Spirit and the Word in their inner lives. Whatever view one takes of the possible speed at which we are capable of developing spiritually, we can all agree that we need to be consciously invested in the process.

The Old Testament provides numerous examples of how people became transformed by God. Living under the covenant meant that one lived consciously in the presence of God ("I will dwell among them" [Exod 25:8; 29:45; Lev 26:11-12; Num 5:3; Deut 12:11; 1 Kgs 6:13; Zech 2:10-11; Ezek 48:35bc]). Examples can be lifted up such as Caleb's "wholehearted dedication" to obeying and trusting God in Deuteronomy 1:36 and Numbers 14:24. God's dwelling with the people implies that the

---

[9]A. W. Richard Sipe, *Sex, Priests and Power: Anatomy of a Crisis* (New York: Brunner/Mazel, 1995).

[10]Cf. the Apostle Paul's description in Galatians 6:14-15 and 2 Corinthians 5:17.

people would be assisted in responding and obeying by God's own Spirit as God empowered them by grace and gifts. Cooperative obedience in reverence for God and the highest respect for other people are transformational forces in any committed Christian community.

In New Testament passages there are opposing terms such as "fornication, impurity vs. purity" *(hagneia* vs. *porneia,* 1 Tim 5:22b: "Keep yourself pure—*hagnos")* which speak to the dedication of self unto God for special relationship and service. These terms have both God-reference and reference to our fellow human beings. This represents a basic stance of the new covenant. Formation for ministry calls us to deliberately commit ourselves to a lifestyle and service that reflects our gratitude to God for grace and calling, while living in such a way as not to do harm to others, but rather to lift others by our example and quality of life and leadership.

The choices we make, the struggle with "the old person" that dwells in each of us, and the need to decide "to put on the new" are part and parcel of our theological-ethical principles of daily life under God that make a transforming ideal part of our whole life-stance toward God and each other (cf. Rom 13:12-14; Eph 4:17-24; Col 3:7-10; 1 Tim 3:1-13; 4:12, 16; 5:1-2, 20-22; 6:14; Titus 1:5-9; 2:1-8, 14-15; 2 Cor 3:17-18). This does not imply perfectionistic "white-knuckling." This represents a glad response of the heart. We prayerfully dedicate ourselves to become changed persons until the day of perfection in the "New Age" of God's perfect presence. To all who so position mind, will, and affections, God's promise is to assist us by the Holy Spirit toward that end (Gal 3:1-5; 4:6-7; 5:5-6, 16, 22-25).

## Family of Origin and Spirituality

There are also some crossovers between spiritual formation and family-of-origin issues. It would be very important to help the seminarian examine questions such as:

1. How did you learn in your family of origin to sense and respect each other's personal boundaries? How does your theological doctrine of the value of each person affect

how you employ that growing adult awareness of boundaries? How does this awareness affect your sense of your own and others' sexual boundaries?

2. How do you clearly present your sexual struggles before God in prayer, and what kinds of resources are you developing from your spiritual repertoire to deal with them? Is there an underlying resentment toward authority that enables you to compartmentalize off into secrecy your sexual lust or fantasy life? For example, when you are at prayer, is one of your parent's faces on the "form" of God? Where do you feel you are not facing this or dealing with this very well, and what reasons might there be for that? What family-of-origin source of toxic shame and accompanying resentment can you identify that continually gets in your way of being spiritually positive and whole?

3. What stage of maturity has your meaningful private and worship prayer life come to? To get a sense of this, how would you classify the involvement of deepest affections and active will in your prayer experience? How is prayer helping you shape your core attitudes toward God and others, and solving your tendency to maintain a self-justifying and idolatrous stance? What exemplary models do you have in mind for this? Where did you get them? Are they working for you?

## Compartmentalization Explained

In closing, we need to deal with one of the most troubling realities, i.e., that persons of faith are capable of compartmentalizing their sexuality from their spiritual convictions. In regard to this issue Richard Sipe pointed us to Robert Jay Lifton's concept of "doubling." Lifton's book *Nazi Doctors* traces how apparently upstanding individuals such as medical doctors could successfully rationalize their misdeeds for long periods under the Nazi regime. Persons who chose a profession such as medicine probably were persons who originally possessed somewhat altruistic motives. Influenced by the ideology and fear-based authority of the Nazi regime, these people were able to compartmentalize their personal ethics in service of the dominant culture and perform heinous and incredible atrocities. Thus, the Nazi "community ethic" overcame their personal ethics. This warns us that we need to recognize the great power church communities have to shape attitudes and values. We can socialize people to be able to either integrate or not their personal values into their daily choices. We must look at ways we shape our ecclesiastical and seminary communities, that is, how we set up the ethos of each community. Are we willing to go beyond simply issuing good sexual harassment and misconduct policies? Are we actively addressing issues that need to be addressed as a regular part of our life together, so that everyone becomes aware of how the cultural attitudes toward sexuality need challenging and replacing with new and better ones?

Compartmentalization is also explained in a helpful way by the "White Book" of Sexaholics Anonymous. This volume is constructed on the "Big Book" model of Alcoholics Anonymous. Their chapter on "The Spiritual Basis of Addiction" describes people who early in their lives came to resent something done to them such as shaming by parents or other authority figures. They then developed an attitude that secretly savored this resentment and justified surreptitiously using sex as a way to rebel while enjoying an intense high in a forbidden area of their lives. This search for sexual intensity gradually takes precedence and control, superseding all other values. These people become fully addicted to resentment as a spiritual attitude quite apart from any physical acting-out. Recovery from such addiction is only possible as a person comes to give up the resentment-motivated attitude and surrenders to the grace of God. True intimacy is impossible until this changed spiritual framework, involving the basic personal attitude and will, is in place.[11] We are at the task of wholesome and integrated spiritual formation and sanctification, leaning on God's grace and assistance, theological integrity, and the necessary education and socialization of our communities of faith.

[11]Sexaholics Anonymous (Nashville: SA Literature, 1989) 49.

## Seminary Education

Increasingly, accrediting associations are requiring seminaries to set up learning outcomes that can be measured and evaluated. We must assess whether we are effectively changing people. We must now show accreditation examiners what students are supposed to learn, and in which area of a student's life the outcomes are to be seen, whether in the cognitive, the affective (motivational, emotional, and volitional), or the concrete practice of ministry. If we apply this philosophy of outcome-based education to the prevention of clergy sexual misconduct, it is necessary to lay out the cognitive, affective, and practical learning objectives that lead us to changes for the better in terms of students' relationships. Some will come to the seminary already quite well along the road to achieving these outcomes and will require little additional help. Others will demonstrate much greater difficulty, even to admit their struggles around these issues, let alone to successfully make good progress toward dealing with them. It is with the latter group that we need to spend our greatest energies and resources. The more healthy group will need monitoring and evaluation, but less educational intervention.

## Further Classifying Outcomes

There are several ways to look at the task of defining our learning outcomes in regard to our interpersonal sexual conduct. First, we would like to ask the reader to step back and get the big picture. Ask: "How do I decide to behave the way I behave?" You might answer immediately that this is a matter of Christian ethics. This answer is partially correct. It is true that our big picture includes a world view, as well as a resulting set of basic ethical principles and their application. However, what makes us decide to act in one way or another in a consistent way over time? Does knowledge of ethical principles suffice? Obviously, it is quite possible for someone to be an expert on ethics and still act in ways that are injurious to others as well as to themselves.

It is difficult to be as consistent as we would love to be. You might be commenting, "Only Jesus . . . ," and you would be right. One of us might be more consistent in the area of application of ethics to broader community issues while others are more alert to interpersonal relationships. The question concerning the best means of lasting change persists. How can we define this process and link those means to the outcomes we really desire and get the results we want?

One approach would be to describe outcomes through focusing on the destructive behaviors that victimize other people and on how to put safety guards around vulnerable people. This focuses more on professional/client boundaries. We look at abuses, damages, the need to take responsibility for maintaining the safety of others. We observe carefully the needed "stop signs" of misconduct. Equity, justice, and safety are primary issues here. This has been the principal approach of Marie Fortune and other pastoral ethicists. Her workshops for clergy describe outcomes in terms of learning how to be aware of both obvious and more subtle abuses of power with someone under our care and thus "hedge against the always-possible misuse of our power."[12]

Another way to define our outcomes is to describe them in terms of the ways we are drawn to cross boundaries when we are in close proximity to an opportunity for that kind of behavior. This would focus on our "love hunger," our inner sexual and emotional health, our ways of feeling alienated and pushed away from or by people with whom we want to relate sexually in order to fill our needs. Included in this would be needed attention to spiritual forces that either are compartmentalized from our sexuality or developing an ability to take care of ourselves in a holistic way so that we would be less prone to transgress the boundaries of other people. This is the psycho-spiritual approach. This might involve family-of-origin work, and counseling, as well as some structured accountability and confidentiality-guarding. Spiritual direction, or what Kenneth Leach calls "a spiritual friend," might be appropriate help in this regard.

A third way to do this is to enrich the cognitive understanding of theological principles involved in interpersonal relationships. We would investigate the background of how we understand

---

[12]Marie Fortune and others, *Clergy Misconduct: Sexual Abuse in the Ministerial Relationship,* educational workshop trainer's manual (Seattle: Center for the Prevention of Sexual and Domestic Violence, 1992).

God's divine purposes for interrelationships, community, individuality, our theological view of women, as well as issues such as wholeness and healing.

A careful study of the divine purposes in creation and redemption for our sexuality would be an irreplaceable piece of this theological understanding. A theology of justice-making in ethical decision making would also be helpful. What is our theology of prayer and communion with God? How does that theology get put into practice and affect our daily behavior?

Outcomes need also to have long-range applicability. One could imagine a student going through all three of these major areas in a fairly thorough way and still not bring it all into a positively weighted integration. This is where the usefulness of the concepts of "spiritual formation" come into play. In spiritual formation attention is given to how well the integration is going, in either small groups or through one-on-one encounters with mature, experienced mentors. This is often a process involving several years and would well include periodic "check-ups" over one's entire life. Since life brings us losses, changes, and challenges which need to be processed and adaptations made to bring us back into balance and health again, we are never totally done with it.

Ideally, each seminary would have an appointed staff or faculty person responsible to check periodically with all students in regard to the above three outcome areas. The difficulty to squarely face in this regard is that seminary personnel need to carefully respect the individual boundaries of the student. However, the student needs to be presented with the needed reviews. Data gathering should be done in such a way as to stimulate a thorough personal self-examination. This is a delicate line to walk. Not only is this delicate material to discuss with students, but it is not always possible for students to know by themselves whether they are entirely healthy or not.

Counselors, including those who do spiritual direction, might ask: "Where and how does this student connect with spiritual resources, and how does the consciousness of God's will for them get brought into fuller, applicable awareness?"

In summary, our layout of outcomes and methods attached to them will have to be broad enough, on the one hand, to touch base with students' world views and basic ethical principles, but personal enough, on the other, to help them monitor specifics having to do with the treatment of others in their professional and interpersonal relationships. All of the above methods need to be combined together for best results. The outcomes might look like this:

In the area of spirituality, a candidate for ministry should be able to develop and demonstrate concretely all of the following cognitive and affective outcomes:

1. A spiritual and theological base for maintaining respect for one's own sexuality, and for persons of the opposite sex, their personhood and personal-sexual boundaries; a clear awareness of both the positive and destructive capacities of our sexual nature.
2. A genuine capacity for intimacy with God, self, and others.
3. A balanced lifestyle that while under spiritual direction/ mentorship implements plans and structures for spiritual self-care that recognize both one's strengths and limits.
4. Gratitude for God's grace and divine calling to ministry.
5. Capacity to resist surrounding cultural influences that degrade and disrespect the sanctity of our sexual nature.
6. Awareness of how our spirituality is influenced by our family of origin.
7. Commitment to one's primary relationships, spouse, and children; examination of the tension between marriage vows and ordination vows.

This chapter has highlighted the role of spiritual formation in a candidate's sexual valuing and resources for dealing with spiritual life and sexual issues. We do not believe that spiritual resources are the only ones to be used. However, it is our conviction that too often in seminary and ordination processes, the spiritual resources that are available to our candidates have been used either very little, to deny problems, or in shaming ways. It is our hope that this chapter has placed the spiritual resources of every theological student in a more positive light.

We shift our attention next to process education and contextual settings where supervision and group experience can help candidates further enhance their ability to integrate their sexual life in healthy directions.

# Chapter Nine

# Field Education and Sexuality Issues

## The Nature of Field Education

Definitions and models of field education used today vary (e.g., "contextual education" is the term often used in about half of the nation's Lutheran seminaries). Indeed, our present-day terminology and practice reflect to some extent the 1970s thinking and effort to put educational experience in context. However, seminaries often follow their own "lights" concerning how to do this. As most alert readers know, there exists a great variety of types of internships, e.g., part-time, field education co-extensive with classroom, as compared to full-time involvement separate from classroom time, and other modifications.

The learning methodology involves process learning, that is, learning what results from active involvement in ministry. This includes regularly structured opportunities for reflection and discussion about the ways students put together a theological understanding of ordained ministry, various ministry methods, and awareness of the use of one's person as a vehicle for ministry. In field education a supervisor works alongside the student and observes and discusses those ministry events and contexts with the student. These parish supervisors seldom have the background of extensive clinical training. Few have as much psychological and methodological sophistication as clinical pastoral education supervisors. In fact, seminaries vary a great deal in how much they prepare their site supervisors or how much they check or evaluate the supervision process.

With all of its weaknesses, field education is seen by most denominational and seminary leaders as valuable and largely effective. Wendell Debner, of the Contextual Education Office at Luther Seminary in St. Paul, Minnesota, found in his research that the church-system context has more emotional content than the seminary context. This means that the student gets challenged immediately to look at church reality from a vantage point very different than that of the emotionally "cooler" classroom. Students often are surprised by this and feel more vulnerable and anxious. With the field education set up to be a hands-on mentoring experience, however, there is the opportunity for stepping back from what feels dangerous and threatening and getting a perspective that functions well. Being in context allows the student to try out ways of doing ministry while getting guidance and feedback from within the unique context itself. Emotional and sexual feelings will be some of the dynamics of this process.

In the midst of this students can be alerted that their sexuality goes with them everywhere. They are never non-sexual beings. Field education provides an opportunity to observe how they feel about this as they go through it and to get information about the way other people see them functioning in that context. While seminaries should deal with sexual issues in the spiritual-formation process, field education is an important check station where, as Debner says, the greater emotional content of the church setting influences more powerfully the sexual feelings of the students.

## Critical Spots in the Field Education Process

Seminaries and church bodies have legal limits concerning the data one can ask directly from students concerning their private lives. On the other hand, some states require criminal background checks on people who will be involved in counseling at any level. However, these background checks are carried out by the church bodies interested in hiring the students, not by the seminaries. In their admissions process seminaries depend more upon reference letters written by pastors and lay people in the students' home churches and during the time the student is on campus. Often students are put through a psychological testing program of varying degrees of thoroughness, often executed by one of a dozen regional career development centers. According to Dr. Francis A. Lonsway, coordinator of student information resources of the Association of Theological Schools, about fifty-four ATS schools use a program called "Profiles of Ministry" that implements a multifaceted evaluation for readiness for ministry.[1]

By and large these practices would not usually pick up on any sexual problems of students, unless there were quite gross indicators on a tool such as the MMPI II. Therefore, it would be important to prepare field-education supervisors and lay committees to watch for clues that students might not be emotionally or sexually healthy.

## Field-Education Clues to Potential Problems

The element of learning about one's sexuality in ministry inherently involves much complexity, ambiguity, and resultant resistance by students. However, there are observable clues to conditions that possibly predispose students to clergy sexual misconduct. Pastoral supervisors and field education directors will want to keep a vigilant eye on these conditions or clues. We will illustrate each condition with a composite vignette.

Under the general heading of "relational skills" one may notice, for example: difficulty perceiving and working comfortably and appropriately with other people's personal "turf" or boundaries; e.g., being invasive/pushy, at one extreme, or extremely isolated and withdrawn and lonely, on the other.

David, a first-year seminarian, has impressed the entire seminary community with the dynamic nature of his personality. Possessing a rich baritone voice, his greetings were loud and effusive. He had the ability to involve himself in any and all conversations. His energy level was always extremely high. Yet, when talking with people, on the one hand he appears enthused about the conversation, but on the other, he does not really seem to be fully present. He often noisily interrupts the conversation of oth-

---

[1]Personal communication, May 29, 1996.

ers. A person's privacy was something for which he showed little respect. His interruptions were always friendly and enthusiastic, so people had difficulty complaining about them. At every opportunity David involves himself with the social life of the seminary, belonging to everything, and appearing at most functions. Yet one does not get the sense that he is involved at a deeply personal level. He knows people's names, and they are impressed that he will probably do well as an intern at the church. While on the one hand, everyone is acquainted with David, on the other, no one really knows him. His energy is generally so strong, people often feel overpowered. So there is no true closeness to others.

Frequently authority issues are involved in David's type of personality, for example: difficulty being balanced and appropriately humble concerning one's need for accountability and interdependence; being angry at "the system" and putting oneself in a victim's role; and blaming others for one's own lack of accountability. This kind of person might sometimes look like "a wheeler and dealer," flitting about with many simultaneous projects, spinning them like the plate juggler. The problem is that this kind of person submits to no one board or ecclesiastical authority. Sexual misconduct and other related offenses may more easily occur in such a life simply because of the personally created and tailored sense of entitlement.

Larry has been placed in a church as a seminary intern. Larry has openly questioned the field-education requirements, and others have often detected a subtle arrogance in him. There seems to be an attitude that he does not need field education because he is ready for ministry. The supervisor notices that he often misses appointments for supervision, sometimes shows up late, and rarely completes written work. When challenged about this, Larry blames his busy schedule and the multiple demands upon his time with his wife and new baby. His fellow students have noticed that Larry spends lots of time complaining about his supervising pastor. His main complaint is that the supervisor does not let him do enough of the more responsible tasks such as preaching. They also notice that in field-education group discussions Larry often will answer other students' questions, giving them advice, but will never ask questions of his own that reveal his own need for input from them.

Underlying emotional neediness ("love hunger") can be sensed by others. A person like Larry tries to meet this neediness by acting "burned out" or by needing exceptional amounts of support. He is not honest with or accountable to his support group. Larry may also try to find intimacy with those he ministers to, crossing appropriate boundaries, instead of building intimacy with normal networks of support.

Stewart, like David, has impressed his field-education setting with the dynamic nature of his personality. He is enthusiastic, warm, and engaging. He often spends extra hours at his church duties, and the senior pastor has to remind him to go home. He seems to thrive on helping with the personal crises of the people with whom he works. People who have spent time with him come to realize that in reality he is not a very good listener. They often feel treated paternalistically. Stewart is more of a teacher even in his counseling sessions. During supervisory sessions, he complains about the schedule, and workload at the seminary and the church. When talking about some of his counseling sessions, he often describes his helpees in sarcastic and demeaning terms. Occasionally he complains about their excessive neediness and the demands they place on his time. However, Stewart would rather do one more counseling session than go to a support group for his own needs. In church meetings he often lectures others on the way things ought to be done, occasionally using biblical references to emphasize his point. He is so outwardly charming and intelligent, along with his high biblical literacy, that people hesitate to argue with him. Yet were he ever to be confronted, Stewart would look back at the person with the eyes of someone who has been personally wounded. Later, behind their back, Stewart will complain about having been misunderstood and criticize the person who had disagreed with him. Newcomers would often react warmly to Stewart, feeling the ingratiating nature of his personality; later, however, they would perceive that they had been manipulated by him.

Persons who use a lot of sexual humor, always looking for double entendre, are testing the waters of other people's willingness to talk about sex. At John's field-education setting, everyone loved his witty dry sense of humor. He is always looking for another chance to crack a joke or make harmless fun out of any situation. Sometimes, however, people in meetings have been frustrated that he never seems to be able to take anything too seriously. His male colleagues have noticed that John will always look for the sexual themes in any conversation, often pointing out sexual double meanings of otherwise nonsexual conversation. Women in the church have noticed a certain degree of sexual teasing and flirtatiousness in him, almost adolescent in its quality. Several women who know him well have reported that he has told sexual jokes, always apologizing for them beforehand, but telling them anyway. His personality is so engaging that they have difficulty in pointing this out to him. John is a warm and friendly person, and loves to give hugs, whether people are uncomfortable with them or not.

Some may seem inordinately interested in a certain population group, but have at the same time underlying anger about it, using put-downs, critical humor, and theological devaluation. This may be a group of people they feel strongly sexually attracted to, but experience anger at them.

Curt is a handsome and dynamic young man and has taken to his role as a leader of the young adults, both married and single. Young women have been drawn to him because of his warm personal style. He is a good listener and seems to be available to them whenever they need him. His supervising pastor has discovered that he has occasionally given his home phone number to some of these women. He has conducted a number of visits with some of them in their homes, and he has seen others at the church in the evening. One of them has told the supervising pastor "Isn't Curt wonderful—he told me to call him, whether day or night!" The young men in this same group report feeling somewhat neglected. One of them even admitted feeling jealous of the amount of time Curt gets to spend with the young women in the group. Curt's fellow male students would report that he is somewhat of a chauvinist, often telling demeaning jokes about women or commenting about women's inadequacies. Curt tells particularly demeaning stories about his mother and sister.

Persons with theological rigidity may reveal a "taut-bow-string" anxiety" factor underneath; they may be defensive and sometimes even controlling. Stan is impressing the seminary community with his ability to quote Scripture. He seems to punctuate most of his discussions with biblical references. In class he will challenge professors who bring up controversial theological points or questions about traditional interpretations of Scripture. People are often impressed with an attitude that "I know God's will, and you don't." His supervising pastor has noticed that Stan is quick to point out the sexual temptations in surrounding culture. He seems constantly to do battle with pornography in a variety of cultural media. He is currently organizing a boycott against a local video store. When challenged on his own sexual temptations, Stan denies that he has any problems. His wife has made an appointment with one of the seminary faculty reporting her loneliness and feelings concerning Stan's coldness. She has also reported his excessive sexual demands, saying he usually quotes Ephesians 5 about women submitting to their husbands.

On the other hand, over-display of personal inner struggles through preaching or teaching may reveal an attempt to thus overcome one's own problems. Ed's supervising pastor became concerned about him after he preached his first sermon. In it Ed referred repeatedly to his relationship with his wife, so much so that people were somewhat embarrassed for her. He claims he was trying to make some points about relationships, but several perceptive people had a feeling that he was reaching out for help. When he teaches, Ed often uses stories from his own past that illustrate the wounds and struggles he has experienced. In several counseling sessions people have reported to the supervising pastor that they usually end up talking as much about Ed as they talk about anything else.

Sexually or emotionally troubled people may demonstrate imbalanced use of the spiritual disciplines (cf. Dallas Willard, *The Spirit of the Disciplines*), along with inconsistency in their personal convictions and feelings about themselves as persons in ministry. Some persons use their faith in addictive ways, i.e., as a means of mood alteration, attempting to compensate for a lack of ability to attain intimacy in appropriate ways with either people or God.

Dan has impressed the seminary faculty that his spiritual life is a matter of extremes. He goes through periods during which he reports to them long hours spent in Bible study and prayer, but reporting them as if documenting hours of work, without a sincere joy, satisfaction, or peace in the experience. His field-education supervisor questions whether he has a spiritual life at all because he often goes through periods of time when he pays no attention to it. The supervisor also notices that Dan prays in public in a way that is usually very formal and stilted. He does not get a sense of a warm, personal investment in prayer.

In cases where we are experiencing some negative clues, we may need to inquire how students are perceived by their support networks. We need especially to watch for any level of narcissism, manipulative tendencies, or evidences that they try to "con" or manipulate others. Such people may have an underlying emotional neediness but not have a balanced interdependence with friends and support groups. They are using the group for their neediness, not for healthy reality checks.

The more these above issues are present, the more reason for concern. Remember that these behavioral factors may point at areas of conflict/need *other than* sexual ones. Only a professional evaluation can determine exactly what the meanings really are.

One might ask: What about students or ministers who simply fall in love with their counselee/parishioner? To what do we attribute most of these cases? Is it simply the "love-hunger" factor? What factor does marital health play in all of this? If students are educated about proper professional boundaries, and yet experience this "falling in love" with someone under their care, it would be necessary to conduct a thorough interview with the student to determine why those boundaries were crossed and what conscious decisions were made in order to understand the dynamics and responsibilities involved with them.

## Ongoing Concerns

As students go through the field education program, we need to follow them up in order to: (a) keep students motivated to value and use the process (rather than feeling they just have to "jump through the field-education hoop"), (b) evaluate their effective integrating of the experience for future change, and (c) keep the field-education process flexible enough to tailor some aspects of it, while still focusing sufficiently on the basic elements of standardized outcomes.

Our well-prepared orientation of students for field education should motivate them to take personal ownership of the important functions of field education in their preparation for ministry. We should ask them to provide us with all the necessary background so that the process is holistically helpful to them, and we should maintain on our part an attitude toward them that balances the policies and outcomes descriptions with encouragement and supportive, non-punitive interchanges.

## Issues for CPE or AAPC Supervision Process

Candidates for ministry often are involved in Clinical Pastoral Education. Many major denominations require it. The nature of CPE supervision and interaction with peers is intensely and personally interactive. Because of this, there are many opportunities for students to examine and learn about their own sexuality and for others to observe and interact with the candidates around issues of sexuality.

If the student applies for a unit or more of Clinical Pastoral Education, the CPE supervisor will do an intake interview designed to (1) get information about the student's readiness for the experience, (2) to determine whether the student fits well into the particular student group a supervisor is in the process of forming, and (3) to interact with the student in a variety of ways to see if the supervisor thinks it is possible to work well with this student. Also, as the student interacts with secretaries and other staff in the office, there is a limited but important opportunity (after the student leaves the office) to test whether anyone feels uncomfortable with this person for some reason.

As a supervisor reads over the student's application materials, there will be important clues as to the student's attitudes, values, and self-awareness. A question could be included in the application concerning the student's agreement to respect all sexual boundaries while working in the institution. Definitions of sexual harassment and misconduct could be included as part of the initial contract agreement. The signing of such a set of definitions could be done with the supervisor present, so as to observe the student's reaction to it. More and more hospitals and nursing care centers are also requiring background checks on all staff.

Reference letters and phone calls are also used by many supervisors to verify the student's character and behavioral patterns. In the process of CPE there is ample opportunity to observe the student in interaction with people of both sexes, whether with staff people, patients, or authority figures of either the CPE or health care system. Many CPE supervisors are now giving an orientation session to students about sexual boundaries and attempting to raise the participants' awareness to ways that state laws and standards of professional ethics are to be observed in the process of caring for vulnerable people. Resistance may be noted during the orientation or, after getting into the quarter unit, certain behaviors may be observed that signal the student's negative attitudes toward guidelines about sexual boundaries. For example, a student may attempt to discount the validity of the guidelines through overt or covert means, e.g., inappropriate joking about them or more covert passive-aggressive stances. It should be standard for all of these observers to have in mind the question, "Do I ever feel uncomfortable around this person, and what do I think the reason for that might be?" Supervisors should check this out concerning all their students and residents on a regular basis. Genuine reasons for concern ought to be communicated to the denominational office that oversees the student's ordination process.

It is much less common for someone not yet ordained to be in the supervisory process of the American Association of Pastoral Counselors. Certification for pastoral counseling is most often sought out by persons who have already served some time in ministry and are, on average, older persons than those in CPE. However, if a candidate for ministry, or a person already in ministry, pursues certification with AAPC, the supervisory process is thorough and not only involves several supervisors over the time-frame of certification but also presents multiple opportunities for observing the candidate's behaviors, values and attitudes, awareness of transference and countertransference, awareness of sexual boundaries, and the kind of bonding that occurs with the supervisors. The only way the supervisor can get at these issues is to observe how the student reports and exhibits attitudes toward clients while dealing with cases. With many AAPC supervisors functioning mostly on a solo basis, with the candidate bringing into their office the reports and tapes of counseling, there is less opportunity to observe directly the student's behaviors and attitudes concerning sexuality issues while with clients.

## Sexual-Integration Outcomes

It would be imperative that each school and church denomination put some energy and thought into formulating desired cognitive outcomes. The question throughout is: "Is this person ready to deal with (1) their personal influence as pertains to sexual feelings, (2) the context of ministry in such a way as to model healthy relationship strengths, and (3) a need for humility concerning their weaknesses?" In this chapter cognitive outcomes need describing in order to gain a grasp of the appropriate parameters of cognition in our candidates for ministry. See the outcomes appendix for the complete outcomes list.

Candidates will be able to demonstrate the following outcomes in their contextual/field education settings:

1. Know the theological and biblical elements of a Christian view of sexuality.
2. Know the interrelationship of the various systems one is a member of, and the role of congregational dynamics.
3. Understand human sexuality and its relationship to personality, dating, marriage, and family.
4. Be informed about gender issues.
5. Be informed about sexual ethics.
6. Grasp and use well relevant counseling ethics, including understanding transference, countertransference, and projection.
7. Follow guidelines for self-care and other-care; how to build and maintain maximal sexual health and respect for self and others.
8. Know how to avoid invasion of others' sexual boundaries.
9. Know and respect the legal, financial, psychological, familial, spiritual, and ecclesiastical consequences of sexual misconduct by persons in ministry; will know consequences as described from the standpoint of primary and secondary victims, or by perpetrators themselves.

Having dealt with the contextual/field education settings and learning process, we will now give attention to community life that candidates need in order to develop the healthiest framework for their expression of their sexuality.

# Chapter Ten

# Community

It is one of the themes of this book that the role of assessment for vulnerability to sexual misconduct is not to exclude people from ministry but to help them heal issues that create this vulnerability. If assessment is achieved early enough in the candidate for ministry's preparation, prevention of sexual misconduct will likely be the result.

A candidate's community is a vital part, both of the assessment process and of the healing process. According to our model of healthy sexuality, community will be part of a candidate's life in which healthy relationship will be practiced. A candidate's ability to be in healthy relationship can be part of the assessment process. Helping a candidate to be in healthy relationship will also be part of the healing process. We believe that participating in healthy community is essential to living a healthy lifestyle.

The term "community" describes many kinds of relationships, and we are again struck by the diversity of training and preparation for ministry that different faith traditions represent. Community includes academic institutions such as seminaries or graduate schools, denominations or religious bodies either as a whole or in part (such as ordination committees), local churches, support group networks, twelve-step fellowships, accountability groups, networks of friends, and marriages and families.

## Community in the Assessment Process

One of our colleagues, Richard Irons, M.D., says that assessing a professional who has sexually offended is a lot like playing basketball one-on-one against Michael Jordan. Jordan is very skilled and will undoubtedly win. Likewise, an offender is very skilled, verbally accomplished, and socially defended. One-on-one, an assessor is easily fooled. However, if a team is assembled, the members can probably pass the ball enough so as to beat even Michael Jordan. An assessment team can also "pass the ball" and not be so easily deceived.

Mark Laaser worked with Dr. Irons in assessing clergy.[1] A team of several professionals were a part of that process: case manager, addictionologist, chaplain, psychologist, and psychiatrist. Professionals being assessed were kept as in-patients for four to five days. Usually at least one female was a part of this team. They often found that different team members elicited different responses from those being assessed. In one particular case a male minister was extremely charming and cooperative with the male members of the assessment team, but he was angry and sexually provocative with the female member of the team. In another case although a minister reported to the team that he never masturbated, a nurse discovered him doing so that night in his room.

When the entire team met for a case review, each team member brought various items of information. These ranged from psychometric testing, social histories, spiritual inventories, addiction screens, and mental status exams. Each team member also brought input from his or her own inter-personal interactions with the client. Individual members of the team also brought their personal observations of and reactions to the patient. When these various pieces were assembled, the resulting picture often portrayed a whole that was different than what each team member would have come up with individually.

We believe that this team concept is important in the process of assessing candidates for ministry. We suspect that many offenders who have "fallen through the cracks" might not have done so if a team approach had been taken. When we first started our work together, we were invited to consult with a church that had recently discovered that a previous pastor had been sued for sexual activity with boys in the parish. This particular priest turned

---

[1]The results of that collaboration have been summarized in chapter two of this book.

out to be one of the more prolific offenders that this diocese had known. This discovery was ten years after the fact. People in the congregation were shocked and amazed. They had considered him to be the finest pastor they had ever had.

We assembled a group of these parishioners for several meetings. Participants ranged from leaders in the church to members of various groups. We began to talk to them about the characteristics of offenders. One by one they began to tell stories that illustrated one of our points. One woman, for example, recalled that this priest used put downs of women in his sermons. Several other women felt that they had been demeaned by this priest. The men recalled statements about loneliness and stress. This group of parishioners assembled a community-wide picture of this priest in which all the pieces fit into a canvas that portrayed a lonely, angry, and socially isolated offender.

What we believe is that candidates for ministry also need to be assessed by a community-wide picture containing pieces of information from a variety of sources. The community in which we believe this is most likely to happen is that of the seminary or training institution and that of the larger denomination. If we use our model of healthy sexuality in chapter six, we can determine what some of these pieces should be. Those who observe the candidate in a variety of settings may contribute various observations if they understand the desired outcomes of the healthy sexuality model.

We think of a seminary student, for example, whose roommate came in for counseling because he was tired of the outbursts of anger that came particularly after this student had been on the phone with his father. This same roommate also disclosed that the student was prone to watching pornography late at night and had a collection of pornographic magazines in his closet. One of this student's professors reported about his rigid, black-and-white theology. The student's advisor was counseling him about a compulsive masturbation habit. The field-education supervisor was troubled by how the student had alienated some of the parents of his youth group. The student health service was frustrated with this student because he complained of many imaginary physical ailments and would not follow their dietary and exercise advice. No one on campus seemed to really know this student because he was a loner.

The challenge represented by such a student is: Whose responsibility is it to collect all of this information and to do something about the picture of a very troubled student? There are various candidates for this role. At the seminary or graduate school level, the student's advisor might be the person. The dean of the school is another. The director of field education also seems possible. At the denominational level there is usually one person who is the chair or director of the formation or ordination process. He or she can delegate the responsibility but could be responsible for it. At the local church level, in those faith traditions where the local church ordains, a board of elders or the existing pastor could assume the role.

One key challenge is how many candidates would this person be responsible for, and how can the information be collected. If the person is responsible for too many people, some will slip through the cracks. Another challenge is that we must remember the individual right of people to privacy and confidentiality. This right must be respected and might at times prevent some from reporting information.

We again look to the broader picture of the community to answer these challenges. One answer is to educate the entire community (seminary, denomination, or church) as to the goal of assembling an assessment picture. This would include education about the healthy sexuality model. This would allow all community members to be more aware of what to look for or be sensitive to. We must be careful not to create a situation of fear, one in which everyone feels that "big brother is watching." Part of the education is that sensitivity to issues is out of love and never out of jealousy or anger.

We cannot emphasize enough the fact that people who become aware of a candidate's risk factors must take responsibility for informing the appropriate denominational authority, namely, the authority who will ultimately be responsible for ordaining or licensing the candidate to practice ministry. For example, too often seminaries have not reported suspicions about a candidate to a denominational authority. Seminary officials might think that to do this would be too judgmental or premature. They have not wanted to destroy a person's career before that person has actually offended. Our belief is that when such reporting takes place, it should not destroy a person's career. Rather, it only allows for the opportunity to heal the risk factors involved.

Perhaps the main reason that reporting does not take place is that there are persons in the system who fear violating anonymity or privacy. The challenge of privacy might be addressed by understanding that ordination is a privilege and not a right. When a person agrees to be in the process of ordination, he or she should also agree to be accountable. This understanding would include the knowledge that certain rights to privacy are voluntarily surrendered to trusted authority. This trust can be earned if the authority has been shown to be operating out of a spirit of love and healing and not out of a spirit of judgment and punishment. We might even suggest that a candidate sign a document agreeing to be in this kind of accountability.

We know, for example, that pastoral privilege of confidentiality does not extend to knowledge of child sexual abuse. Confidentiality does not extend to therapists who have a knowledge that their clients might harm themselves or others. Likewise, should confidentiality extend to the knowledge that there exists a vulnerability to commit sexual misconduct or abuse of self or others? We think not.

When we speak of the community of the seminary, denomination, or local church we are obviously talking about all the member of those communities. We would like to make a special plea that spouses of candidates for ministry be included in those communities. So often, a spouse is aware of warning signs in his or her wife or husband before anyone else is.[2] It might simply be a matter of distance in the relationship. Spouses can be educated about these warning signs and the appropriate measures to take if they perceive there are problems.

Partners of sex addicts have also been shown to suffer from high levels of abuse.[3] Eighty-one percent have experienced sexual trauma, 75 percent physical trauma, and 91 percent emotional trauma. Educating spouses about abuse and the appropriate help

---

[2] Cf. Mark Laaser, *Faithful and True: Sexual Integrity in a Fallen World* (Grand Rapids, Mich.: Zondervan Publications, 1995) 75, the warning signs of sexually addicted pastors.

[3] Cf. Patrick Carnes, *Don't Call It Love: Recovery from Sexual Addiction* (New York: Bantam Books, 1991) 146.

that is available is an important part of decreasing vulnerability. We know that it is important for both partners of a marriage in which sexual addiction is an issue to get individual and marriage counseling to deal with the effects of the abuse in the relationship (cf. M. Laaser's article in the *Journal of Sex Addiction/Compulsivity* [Fall 1996]). Marital distress is a factor in vulnerability to sexual misconduct, and this issue must be addressed. It is highly likely that any candidate for ministry that is vulnerable to sexual misconduct, sexually addicted or not, has a spouse who will have issues of his or her own with which to deal.

## The Community as a Source of Healing

When an assessment is made that a candidate for ministry is vulnerable to sexual misconduct, the community of the seminary, denomination, and/or local church can be instrumental as a source of healing. Several factors are important. Does the community have an attitude of healing, love, forgiveness, and restoration? Does the community believe that it is safe to allow a person with known vulnerability to enter ministry if they are well? Do they have the resources of money, personnel, and clinical experience? Is someone leading or at least responsible for the process?

Also key is whether or not the communities themselves are healthy enough to be healing. Sadly, we recognize that not only are some communities not sources of healing but they may also contribute to vulnerability. It is our experience, for example, through many stories from students and faculty members alike that the incidence of sexual relations between faculty and students at various seminaries is quite high. This can be true both homosexually and heterosexually. Mark Laaser, for example, has talked to several Catholic seminarians who were sexual with various spiritual directors and supervisors along the route of their training. One of these went on to abuse young boys. He also has talked to a number of female seminarians who report either being sexual abused or sexually harassed by faculty and supervisors during their training. (Marie Fortune says approximately 50 percent of female seminarians have been sexually harassed.) We both have also known many stories of denominational officials, at various levels, who have been sexually involved with others, including candidates for ministry. It is not an uncommon story for supervising pastors to have been sexual with interns.

Church congregations as an entire system can be unhealthy and not particularly healing. We know one congregation that over a one-hundred-year history called eight successive pastors, all of whom were guilty of sexual misconduct. This is not coincidence; there was something about the congregation that either attracted or needed this type of pastor.

Ultimately, each candidate for ministry must be responsible for his or her own progress toward healing. Each seminary and church denomination or local congregation must be responsible for its own health. A student must be educated as to what a healthy community is like in order to make a healthy choice about what group he or she should pursue ministry in. A denomination or church must examine itself and strive to be a healing community.

Following are some suggestions for what a healthy community might provide to the healing process of a candidate for ministry:

- Safety from sexual abuse and harassment.
- Support of spouses, including equal access to counseling and support activities.
- Individual and marriage counseling opportunities.
- Social events.
- Worship experience opportunities.
- Marriage-enrichment seminars.
- Sponsors or mentors to new candidates and spouses.
- Child care.
- Approaches to isolated singles that help them get integrated.
- Testing and measurement availability in early stages that includes marriage assessment.
- Information about, support for, and access to twelve-step and other support groups.

It will be challenging for any candidate to maintain a schedule of work, academics, social and family life, much less to include any of the opportunities for growth listed. This is stressful. It is also the challenge of being in ministry and being and staying healthy. If a candidate is not able to successfully negotiate this challenge while preparing for ministry, how will they deal with the stresses of ministry later?

As mentioned in our first section, the more people talk to each other about a candidate for ministry, the more likely a complete and accurate picture will be created. The challenge is to find those who will be responsible for assembling this picture. Likewise, there must be people who will be liaisons or bridges between academic training institution, denominations, and local churches such that a unified healing community is created. Duplication of effort can tax limited resources. "Turf" issues distract from the ultimate goal. Theological differences may also create sidetracks. Variations are great from church/denomination to church/denomination. Schools vary in degree of association with church bodies. Nevertheless, the best available connections should be encouraged and monitored.

The ordination process and its relationship to the school/ church body should be structured in ways that bring students into a healthy, positive accountability and support networks. This, in the best sense, is what should be meant by being "under care" of a particular denomination or religious body. This process should be encouraging and not discouraging, a genuinely integrating experience and not just a series of hoops to be negotiated. Finally, it should be safe for a candidate to deal with sexuality issues in the midst of his or her process.

## Community Outcomes

Candidates for ministry who are relatively healthy and who have participated in a healthy community will demonstrate certain characteristics:

1. Active in their local church.
2. Regular social event participation.
3. Knowledge of and use of support systems.
4. Participate in study, accountability, and support groups.
5. Active in student affairs.
6. Knows how to balance solitude with social life.
7. Marriage relationship strong and healthy.

8. Support of family of origin and healing around family of origin issues.

9. Respect for one's own and for others' boundaries.

The next chapter summarizes all the learning outcomes under a single heading for a unified grasp of the entire preparation process.

# Conclusions

Part Two of this book has aimed at describing the ways candidates for ministry can be taught and supervised so as to increase the possibility of preventing sexual misconduct. We have outlined cognitive, spiritual, supervisory, and community formation involved in the prevention of such injurious actions. This chapter aims at coordinating all the outcomes in a unified and easily used list.

With the increasing emphasis in the Association of Theological Schools on definition of outcomes for seminary education, we have thought it important to delineate a set of educational outcomes for the reader to consider for implementation. This list is not exhaustive, nor are all the categories spelled out as fully as they could be. However, in your own schools, preparation for ordination, or in the ways you lift up the ideals you are aiming for in your own ecclesiastical tradition, we would hope this list will stimulate you to think through carefully some appropriate goals and the means you use to reach them.

We follow here the commonly employed divisions of educational outcomes, (1) cognitive, (2) affective, and (3) action-specific. The first has to do with the intellectual content of learning, the second with the area of value-laden appreciation and conviction, and the third with concrete results in life as they are lived out in community.

## Cognitive Outcomes for Prevention of Sexual Misconduct

Upon completion of preparation for ministry, the candidate will demonstrate a reasonably complete grasp of the following:

1. The theological and biblical elements of a Christian view of sexuality.
2. The interrelationship of relevant family-systems concepts.
3. Human sexuality and its relationship to personality, dating, marriage, and family.
4. Gender differences and perceptions of boundaries; how to avoid invasion of others' sexual boundaries; how to share power with other people.
5. The difference between different levels of intimacy and the appropriate boundaries between them.
6. Basic principles of sexual ethics.
7. Relevant counseling ethics, including concepts of transference and countertransference.
8. Guidelines for self-care and other-care, that is, how to build and maintain maximal sexual health while incorporating all relevant spiritual, theological, and social guidelines.
9. The legal, financial, psychological, familial, spiritual, and ecclesiastical consequences of sexual misconduct by persons in ministry; consequences as described from the standpoint of primary and secondary victims, or by perpetrators themselves;
10. The power of the ministerial role.

## Affective Outcomes for Prevention of Sexual Misconduct

By demonstration of values, feelings, and appreciation, students will demonstrate the following outcomes:

1. Clarity and comfort concerning their own sexual identity and sexual preference.
2. A sense of true calling to ministry that is appropriate to one's own spiritual traditions and untrammeled by family agendas; gratitude for God's grace and divine calling to ministry.
3. Non-invasive, yet respectful empathy and sensitive concern for others and their well-being, whatever their age, gender, marital, or mental status.

4. Positive convictions concerning the highest standards of healthy sexuality in all areas of their relationships.

## Action Outcomes for Prevention of Sexual Misconduct

By their actions, candidates for ministry will demonstrate the following outcomes:

1. Written formulation of a theologically sound and personally integrated view of Christian sexuality.
2. Written description of structures and policies for creating and maintaining safe churches and communities, family life, and personal friendships that will carry out inner convictions concerning both the sanctity and vulnerability of all persons' sexuality. This will be supported by written plans for carrying out the establishing of "safe churches."
3. Written testimony from friends, colleagues, supervisors, and mentors that the student is successfully living a life of integrity in all the areas of sexuality.
4. Capacity for intimacy with God, self, and others.
5. A balanced lifestyle that while under spiritual direction/mentorship implements plans and structures for spiritual self-care that recognize both one's strengths and limits.
6. Capacity to resist surrounding cultural influences that degrade and disrespect the sanctity of our sexual nature.
7. Description of awareness of how our spirituality is influenced by our family of origin.
8. Participation in their local church.
9. Regular social event participation.
10. Knowledge of and use of support systems.
11. Participation in study, accountability, and support groups.
12. Participation in student life while in college and seminary.
13. Evidence of balance of solitude with social life.
14. Support of family of origin and healing around family origin issues.
15. A healing process for any early life trauma.

16. The capacity to be intimate and have healthy attachments and bonds.
17. Healthy primary and secondary relationships, including marriage and friendships.
18. Sobriety from any addictive or unhealthy behaviors.
19. Healthy ability to be in touch with and express feelings.
20. Appropriate physical self-care.

The overall approach in this book has been to emphasize both the internal processes of the individual candidate and the external processes of education and field training. It is obvious that we cannot force anything upon people. We can only invite them to consider the possible contributions of their past and their value system upon their lives and their potential for trouble. As we observe the candidate interact with the information and their expressions of conviction and valuing during the entire educational and preparatory process, we can only hope for opportunities to bring to their attention possible needs for therapy, inner healing, or a more challenging and deep reorientation of attitude. This means that every ecclesiastical or seminary staff person involved with candidates should have some knowledge of the overall issues for them and be alert to ways to gently but firmly encourage the candidate to work on them.

What hope can we hold out to the reader? Sexual misconduct cannot be totally eliminated. This book points you in the direction of reduction of future misconduct by candidates for ministry. Ultimately, all readers must seek to employ the guidelines of this book for themselves. Every ecclesiastical body will need to study and modify our suggestions according to the theological and polity guidelines they prefer to use. Most importantly, we must each commit ourselves to do our best in this regard and make solid progress toward preserving our churches from the extensive damages that are currently occurring. We pray that the implementation of these means will bring greater health and safety to our churches and families, with increased glory to God.

# A Case Study

The following case will serve well to test your understanding of the characteristics of a candidate for ministry who ends up perpetrating on female clients. This man went through seminary and revealed some of his struggles to professors and church officials.

As you read the case, refer back to chapter three to note the possible categories he would have been classified under. Discuss your perceptions with colleagues who have also read the case, and ask the following questions:

1. At what points in this man's life could significant help have been provided to help him avoid getting into trouble?
2. If he were to appear in your seminary or ecclesiastical system as a candidate for ministry, what would you look for, and what would you do with such a person?

The case was written by the person described, but anonymously. We want to express our thanks to him for sharing his story and for desiring to help us all understand better how to be more effective seminary and church leaders.

## Pastor, Addict, Child of God
### Lonely as a Way of Life

In my desk lies a tattered black-and-white photo depicting a country road flanked by miles of unfenced fields which surrounded the farm I was raised on. Vast stretches of uncultivated fields became my only playground. It was as though the landscape of my early childhood reflected the "inscape" of my psyche, barren and lonely. I did not even know another child until I was several years old. My associations with adults, especially my parents, were limited by the constant demands of the farm. So, I roamed the fields, wondering about the names of all the wild flowers I became friends with. I was lonely but did not know the difference.

This constant loneliness, exacerbated by the perpetual busyness of my parents and their emotional unavailability to me, laid the first layer of vulnerability in my life. My father, I now see, carried around a considerable anger and rage, which neither he nor I to this day understand. At times I was victim to verbal abuse and rage, but I could only understand that as my own failure to "be a good boy." Every time he exerted authority over me, I came to resent authority a little more. In time I learned to compensate for that by finding a way to earn acceptance as a model student, intellectual, and people pleaser. Apparently, somewhat the same was true of my need for a nurturing mother. Mine had all the right intentions but lacked time and skills. These experiences led me to two important vows I silently made to myself by the time I was a teenager. One, I would find the woman—girlfriend first and later wife—who would offer me all the warmth, trust, attention, and intimacy I lacked in my lonely childhood. Two, I would become an authority so that I did not have to humiliate myself submitting to higher authorities who were in fact inferior to me.

The day I turned sixteen I bought my own car with money I had saved up from raising pigs. That same day I called a girl for my first date. Dating during high school and college consisted of searching for true intimacy but always within the bounds of appropriateness and virginity. Those boundaries were intact and endured until the time of my marriage when I was only nineteen. I got married as a sophomore in college, no doubt to satisfy my first goal in life. Finding true intimacy with the woman who would give herself completely to me and I to her seemed easy at first. She was extremely bright, vulnerable from the recent death of her father, and seemed as though she needed me as much as I needed her. We were virgins and highly inexperienced, but our sexual relationship proved quite satisfactory at first. I do recall, however, that our honeymoon was cut short by a severe bout with abdominal cramping so painful that I returned to my college medical facility and sought a doctor's help. He asked if I were making "a normal adjustment to married life" and if things were all right between my wife and me. Having no framework of what "normal" might be, I replied that everything was fine. We had, however, had a serious fight which involved her feeling unimportant to me. Perhaps the sharp pain in my belly was an early warning sign of troubles to come.

By this time I had experienced both an evangelical conversion experience and a calling to full-time Christian ministry. The hard-working, over-achieving side of me made me into a model student Christian, always leading Bible studies and volunteering for 5 a.m. prayer vigils. I loved the disciplines of Christian life and wanted to lead others in observing them. I was proud to be a Christian leader, and pride was always an issue with me. The man under whose ministry I came to Christ saw this more clearly than anyone. When I enthusiastically told him of my assurance of my calling through a scriptural passage that literally fell on to me when a Bible toppled off my night stand while I was praying, he did not join in my runaway emotions. Rather, he challenged me to pray some more and find out what lowliness and humility God might want of me:

> I, therefore, a prisoner for the Lord, beg you to lead a life worthy of the calling to which you have been called, with all lowliness and meekness, with patience, forbearing one another in love, eager to maintain the unity of the Spirit in the bond of peace (Eph 4:1-2).

I was stunned. He confronted me instead of congratulating me. He was the first person not to be taken in by my people-pleasing talent for inducing praise and respect.

During college I received several awards and scholarships, eventually being offered a fully paid four-year seminary education leading to a doctorate in ministry. Meanwhile, I served a country church during college where my most severe challenge was an authority conflict with my senior pastor. In many ways, accepting the appointment to work with him was like being sent home to my father again. He was a former military chaplain who loved military authority and exercised domination, intimidation, and control over most church activities and decisions. This was my first role model of a pastoral ministry.

Within a year, I managed to get into a situation with him where I challenged his authority with the authority of our denomination. Ironically, the senior pastor who raged over my insubordination was soon removed from his post and entered a mental health unit for lengthy treatment. At first this seemed the result of all the energy he expended maintaining such a rigid, controlling grip on me and his congregation. What I did not yet know was that he had just been exposed for keeping a secret liaison with one of the widows in the congregation! When I found out and shook my head in disbelief, in no way could I have imagined that years later others would be shaking their heads over me in the same way.

Within a month I was out of that situation, headed for seminary as an Entrance Scholar with my awards and recommendation of the congregation I had just served. While en route, I stopped in for an initial interview as a youth pastor at a larger metropolitan church. They offered me the position almost immediately. Everything was going right for me. I felt I had the world by the tail—everyone respected my calling, my ideas, and my excellence in academic work. I was off to study the depths of Christian faith and belief, to become a doctor of ministry, and to lead those who had ears to hear to the deeper truths of God. How could I have known I was truly off to lose my life so that later, humbled, I might find it?

A number of important emotional events happened that first year in seminary. I had another authority conflict with the new senior pastor over his way versus my way of doing things. Again, my seminary professors intervened and showed me I simply was dealing with a man who had a controlling personality and that I would be better off with a different mentor. By now, a pattern was being established that I would win people's confidence over as a bright, reasonable, and very democratic leader so that as time went on, professors, therapists, and denominational leaders respected me and gave me the benefit of the doubt if ever any conflict or dispute arose. I usually presented myself as the innocent observer of someone else's injustice, so they typically found fault with the other parties involved. I received the seminary faculty's imprimatur when they selected another student and me as the top of our class to represent our seminary on a national tour of the boards and agencies of our denomination. That was a heady experience, and I used that opportunity to write ahead and make contacts with many other influential leaders, thus furthering my status as someone to watch in the future.

That same year I met with the denomination body responsible for ordained ministry to have them approve me for the first level of ordination. When one of them questioned why he saw some Bs on my seminary transcript after my having nearly all As in college, my pride was wounded on the spot. I became defensive and indignant, replying those came from summer graduate courses in English where I was competing not with "mere" seminarians but with advanced Ph.D. candidates. I went on to argue that the problem in the ordained ministry was a semi-literate clergy and few with any real life-changing commitment to Christ! My wife later told me that by the time she entered for her interview, I was raising my voice at them and appeared angry. With the intervention of one of my professors on the committee, who must have made excuses for my brashness as a youthful enthusiasm that would mellow, they narrowly voted me in by a vote or two.

That first year in seminary I was exposed to a number of new ideas about relationships which were circulating in the seminary culture of the seventies. There was talk about "open marriage," which some mature faculty and their wives allegedly had practiced. One or two student couples were reported to be trying this lifestyle, and there were usually rumors circulating about their recent forays beyond monogamy. None of this made much difference to my wife and me at the time, except that it planted an idea in my psyche that was later to receive endorsement from the permissive if not sinful side of me; namely, that it might be permissible to receive intimate emotional gratification elsewhere than from one's spouse. I recall fantasizing what those other couples might be finding they had missed in their marriage as though the "special friend" would bring a forbiddenness and mystique to the experience.

During that first year of seminary, the boy who had been lonely on the farm, the one who never had access to playmates, and the one who grew up stuffing his feelings did not realize how he isolated himself from community life until one day there was to be a private retreat by invitation of one of his professors he esteemed most. He was not invited, and later when he asked about the retreat, he was told, "I didn't think you would have been able to go. You're always so involved in your studies or the church work that we never see you at our informal gatherings, so I didn't believe you went in for that sort of thing." I was shocked at this image of myself. Nearly two decades later I would hear others' views of me back in seminary as they related the career of one who had so much promise but had fallen in his own isolation:

> You were so bright and preoccupied. I always admired you from a distance. I'd see you going across the campus toward the library, but most of us were intimidated to talk with you. We thought you were above us, always working on some theological problem that we would be hard put to discuss with you.
>
> Do you realize how many clergy are afraid to talk with you? Yes, afraid. Your words are so slick and smooth that others fear getting manipulated or taken along for a ride on some agenda that is not theirs. They admire your intellect but are afraid to deal with you emotionally because at that level you are practically unapproachable.

During seminary, then, I was not unlike the little boy pondering wild flowers alone in the fields. My "friends" were select professors whom I admired for their rigorous thinking and a few classmates who were going on to become professors themselves. I was, I am told, emotionally distant and found it very hard to reveal much of my inner struggles, except where that was part of the academic requirement, that is, to participate in one sensitivity training group and report on a crisis counseling session with a parishioner.

The existence of a required sensitivity training group, which as I recall was also to serve double-purpose as a spiritual-growth group, meant my seminary was truly interested in developing the whole person for mature ministry. The inevitable question arises:

What else might they have done to help me become aware earlier of the raging addict developing within?

I am unable to answer whether more psychological tests would have foretold my inherent spiritual weakness (for this was truly a spiritual and not just a moral problem). I leave that to those who know the psychometrics of newer tests far better than I. I suppose the issue of honesty would need to be evaluated carefully. I was so bent on presenting such an image of myself, an image I came to believe in so much as to accept as the truth about me, that I would have answered many questions from the standpoint of that idealized self and would have been quite fearful of exposing any weaknesses toward things sexual. In fact, I would often argue morally against the promiscuousness of other seminarians and men in general perhaps to distract from those same possibilities within me.

Two events might have at least given me foreknowledge of what could be dangerous to me. First, if only we had known what sexual addiction was and could have discussed it in pastoral counseling classes and have heard firsthand from a pastor who could identify him- or herself as a recovering sex or romance addict, I probably could have sought out that person privately and asked them about some of my own feelings.

Instead, what in fact happened was just the opposite. In pastoral-counseling classes, we were exposed to films used for sex therapy which showed a male and a female actor in the live process of learning how to enhance their sexual contact with one another! I did ask for the name of the therapist most involved in that kind of therapy and made an effort to contact him to see if he would concur there was something missing and necessary for my married sexual life. He only dealt with abnormal cases, and mine was not, so I was then left wondering, "Where would you find a woman like the one on that film, so open and available to make you feel fulfilled?"

Second, if it had been possible to form a trusting relationship with someone whom I could identify with in terms of my secret preoccupation with sexual or romantic fulfillment, I might have opened up to him and, had he been in recovery himself, I believe it is possible God might have used him to give me the spiritual tools I needed to avoid my eventful moral collapse.

In other words, the seminary, might have made it possible to acknowledge my developing problem and provided a safe place and person (not someone responsible for grading, evaluating, or otherwise recommending me for ministry) with whom I could confine and seek help. One might ask, Why not the pastoral counseling staff? Much of my work with therapists, as I look back over twenty years of therapy was dishonest, stealth therapy. By that I mean that I carefully guarded which issues I could bring out, even in ongoing, seemingly trusting relationships over years of client contact. My disease remained a non-presenting problem, or if I did discuss it, as I came to do frequently, I certainly minimized it to where it looked more like a growth issue than a tragic personality dysfunction. In fact, I remember once going to a new therapist and announcing that I had a personality disorder of a sexual kind and being argued out of that diagnosis in favor of clinical depression!

During my second year in seminary my wife and I began to experience dysfunction in our relationship. She felt lonely when I studied five days a week and pastored nearly all weekend. She said she felt the church was my mistress and resented it. We sought counseling from one of the professors of pastoral counseling. He tried to help us communicate more of our true feelings with one another. Somehow it came up that my wife felt I spent more time with certain women around the church than I did with her. She was asked whether she felt I was attracted to them and why I might be. Now, the truth was I was beginning to be attracted to them as women and to their emotional openness, which was helpful to me and helped me open up as well. During our counseling the issue was made my wife's issue. "Do you believe he can be attracted to other women and yet be faithful to you?" She replied in controlling terms that set off alarms within me, "No, anyone who is married should not be attracted to anyone else." He asked, "Do you see any difference between being attracted and acting on that attraction? Attraction is just a feeling. Feelings are what they are. It's what we do with them that matters."

I felt affirmed, vindicated, and even liberated. I had it on the most respected authority that it is acceptable and a normal human trait to feel attracted to other women as long as I did not act on it. Our marriage seemed to get along better for a year or two. I graduated and went immediately into a second doctoral program in theology for my Ph.D. so that I could teach seminary, a position more befitting someone who wanted not just to be a pastor but a leader in the theological community. We postponed having any children because we "wanted to see" how our marriage would do first (another dangerous contemporary idea I am sure we picked up from the occasional seminary couple who "outgrew" one another, divorced, and went on to a partner more on his or her level of growth) and have me complete my graduate education.

## Making New Rules and Crossing Boundaries

As I look back with scrupulous honesty, I see several early warning signs of impending near moral failures. At first I began to talk with other students' wives a bit more than was common, dropping by to leave off books and staying for some conversation, wanting them to reach out to me emotionally. Then, my research position took me far away to a workshop in another country. In that workshop I was drawn to a vulnerable, spiritually questing woman. Once, we spent a whole mealtime sitting alone in the workshop room discussing our neediness and isolation from our spouses. I believe that had that time been a little longer and the opportunity a little more private, we could have became sexually involved, much to our own guilt and shame. My boundaries were slipping. My lust to be accepted and "taken in" to a woman's self and body was greater than my will to set definite boundaries. My boundaries, sadly, were situational.

Not more than two months after returning home, I was teaching an introductory course at a nearby college and became attracted to a rather voluptuous woman student. To make matters worse, she submitted a very suggestive paper on an unassigned topic involving the relation between spirituality and the female capacity to be multi-orgasmic. As needy as I was emotionally, that was more than I could handle. With no one I could trust and no male friends whom I would confide in without feeling deep shame, I made the decision on my own to invite this student to discuss her paper with me "after class." She proved to be a flirty, flamboyant woman who had written the paper to get a reaction from me. Soon, we continued to discuss over coffee and in walks in the park not only the paper but the need for healthy individuals to express themselves sexually. In this "testimonial woman" (a term in current vogue at the time which meant a woman who attested to and affirmed our masculinity) I had perhaps for the first time made a "connection" with the dreams and fantasies I had nurtured of being needed and sought after by a woman who could give totally of herself sexually and emotionally.

Within weeks of beginning these private discussions, we made arrangements to spend an evening together. I recall the fear and near panic I felt over what I knew to be crossing a tremendous moral boundary and cultural taboo, but my intense preoccupation with finding out what a woman's total sexual response might be was even greater. Both of us suffered such conflicted feelings that we were not free emotionally to experience anything like the intense act we had imagined. It would have, in fact, felt disappointing had it not been for all the rush of adrenaline just to get there and be together alone.

Once that boundary had been crossed, there was no turning back, and many times in the years to come I would regret ever having broken what felt like a cultural hymen. That boundary had been securely intact for the first twenty-six years of my life. Once crossed, however, it would be too easy to do so again and again. I would later liken that event and its psychic enormity to the cosmic proportions of having violated a natural law and standing now outside of where humans were supposed to dwell. My culture alone did not tell me this; it came from my study of literature. My intellect compared it to Macbeth and King Lear, who murder and discover through their hubris and their pride, they have become tragically and fatally separated from the natural world and cannot find their way back. As Hamlet says, "Things are disjoined." The dead walk around haunting their perpetrators, the blood stains of sins will not wash out, trees in the woods move, hiding violent retribution. Soon, however, I rationalized away that appropriate guilt with the writings of theologians of the 1970s who were espousing the sexual revolution as the true freedom to enjoy God's gift of human sexuality. Their work provided fuel for my feelings of entitlement, that by human rights I was entitled to experience these things. I even shared one of those newly published works with the testimonial woman, just to provide a context of propriety for what we were doing. Still, immediate and irreversible consequences fell upon me more like Shakespeare's tragic hero than my adopted model of the sexually liberated male of the seventies.

Death came almost immediately. The very moment I walked in the door from that illicit encounter my marriage died. My wife confronted me, asking exactly where I had been. Instinctively, my fear and protection mechanisms offered a lie. I heard myself saying that I had been at the evangelism committee meeting until quite late. That was a last, gasping breath. Earlier that evening, out of concern for my safety, she had phoned the chairperson asking if I were still there. He of course replied that I had never been there. Angrily and quite perceptively she charged, "You've been with another woman, haven't you?" I was found out, and there was no hiding the truth. Trapped in my own lie, I admitted it. She threw her wedding ring across the room in a rage, and though in the years to come we tried to reconcile several times, nothing quite could restore the bond I had broken that night, especially because I did not really change except to become more discreet and careful in the details of my alibis and my lying.

The next day more of my world was thrown into turmoil. Some of my seminary colleagues and my pastor sought me out to ask if we did not need help. An emergency counseling appointment was set for that night. I felt this would be a good time to have a respected professional validate my reasons for turning to another woman. Though that session is now nineteen years in the past, I will never forget two moments from it. The first came after I had made my case justifying my actions. He grew more enraged than I thought any professional should and challenged me, saying, "I've never heard so much play acting in this office in my life! Never!" I felt betrayed, exposed, misunderstood. Academic colleagues are supposed to stand together and support one another. He was supposed to side with me as victim, but he refused to. Second, my wife and he both said I would have to give up seeing this woman before he could help. I refused to do so, and my reason still rings in my ears with all its delusion: "No, she really loves me." The promise of total sexual fulfillment was too great to risk losing so soon after the conquest of finding it. The truth was, as was usually the case with such affairs, within two months she and her illusory love were completely gone. She quickly proved to be uncommitted and even emotionally un-available, but not quite before she also proved the thesis of her paper, which proof only made me more sure I needed that powerful experience on a regular basis as a fulfillment of the unloved side of me. Today, I remain convinced the power of such lust to numb the will and normal moral thinking is no less, and probably greater than, the effect of drugs such as cocaine and heroin. Only lust is more immediately available and lasts longer.

I returned to work with that therapist by myself for about a year and again five years later when my acting out became more unmanageable. I have often wished he had continued the con-frontational style he risked that first night and had suggested more limits to my behavior so that I could have discovered my powerlessness over it sooner. As time went on and I persisted in my behavior, he would discuss its danger and undesirability but never its progressive and fatal nature. He never again asked me to stop but rather to cut down its frequency as I found more healthy expressions for having my needs met. Never there nor in any other therapy with several other counselors did the words "compulsive," "addictive," or "illness" come up in reference to my acting out. We approached it more as an undesirable activity that would be managed by increasing insight into my fears and hidden emotions. That was precisely the limiting point; we were always attempting to manage the power of lust but not confront and withdraw from it. Hence, I continued into a progressive spi-ral of disassociation from myself, my colleagues, and everyone close to me.

What follows in my story is a ten year period of affairs, three other marriages, and a complete moral failure in my life, result-ing in my being asked to leave the ordained ministry after seven years of local church ministry.

One day, five years after I left my ministry, I admitted for the first time to a clergy friend, "My life is not working. In spite of my prayers and counseling, things really haven't changed, and I can't get out of this mess I continually create." That was the ad-mission of powerlessness that qualifies one to embark on a twelve-step program of recovery. And a twelve-step program is exactly what my friend directed me to, witnessing how his own life had been turned around by such a group. A year into that program, an announcement was made about a workshop for former clergy in recovery from sexual addictions. I had never heard of "sexual addiction," but it sounded exactly like what I had experienced.

At that workshop I heard a man speak who claimed to have been freed from compulsive relationships and sexual addiction for fifteen years. He was the founder of one of the twelve-step programs that had grown out of Alcoholics Anonymous for those with sexually-related addictions. His story was shocking and far worse than my own behavior, but I identified with so much of what he said, I knew I had to get into one of those groups, and so I did the very next day. Months into that program of recovery, I was sober and I was getting better, but thoughts kept coming back to my mind about the last woman I had just left before marrying my then current wife. I lost my sobriety twice during my first six months in the program, each time acting out with the woman I had recently lived with. During that time I thought, as many others have thought to the detriment of their program, that I could stretch the rules and find an easier, softer way to recover.

For me, in the end there was no other way than complete sexual abstinence from myself and anyone I was not married to. I had to dry out and let all the addictive toxins be purged from my system. This toxicity kept suggesting I must have someone there to be mother and confidant, but in a new strategy I kept telling those fantasies and cravings to men in the group instead. After many breakfasts, lunches, and going out to coffee after meetings with this newly-found fellowship of sobriety, I gradually discovered I was not going to die without my drug. Meanwhile, I learned to write down my responses to each of the twelve-steps and share them with a sponsor, a chosen sober member who held up reality for me and helped me face my fears and resentments.

One of the spiritual highlights of my recovery was the day my sponsor helped me do my Fifth Step. This is a special time to meet to tell God, yourself, and another human being the exact nature of your wrongs in the form of a moral inventory of yourself. Here was the antithesis of my former acting out, which had been largely carried out alone with someone in a room off by ourselves somewhere. On the day of my Fifth Step, much as I previously would have done for a lover, but now for God, I ritualistically vacuumed and cleaned a room for the occasion. I opened the windows to let in fresh air, put a vase with a beautiful bouquet of flowers on the table with my Bible and other reading materials, and supplied us with ample fresh fruit and pure water. We spent the better part of the day in there together, but when we emerged, it was like my baptism all over again. I felt assured there was no turning back and that God's grace had reclaimed me from the powers of darkness that previously held me captive.

That was several years ago. I have not only remained sober and completely free from the compulsion even to flirt or speak suggestively to other women for five years now, but I have begun to deal with the painful character defects that caused my isolation and acting out. Through accountability to a sponsor in the program, I have repeatedly learned hard lessons of humility and a new way of letting myself be guided by another's authority over me. I have found individuals and meetings who are not beguiled by any of my clever posturing. They call me on my self-deception, and when my wounded pride and rage has settled, they help me assess what needs changing in my life.

Through developing new, appropriate relationships with men in the groups I attended, eventually healing came between me and my parents, who had been deeply hurt by my moral failures. With my father, I had to get to the point of being able to tell him of my humbling weakness and of my utter trust in God not to abandon me when I had abandoned all else. We had an immediate and overwhelming Father and Prodigal Son reunion experience, hugging and kissing each other until my mother, too embarrassed to know what to do, tried to get us to stop! Today, my father carries a burden and prays for other "brothers" in my program.

Today I enjoy five years of continuous sobriety and recovery from romance addiction. Many other aspects of my life have now come into balance. My eating and exercise habits have changed dramatically. I feel healthier now than at any earlier time in my life. I have remarried and now love my wife wholly with no other distractions. She and I carry the message of my past and recovery to as many other pastors, spouses, and lay people as have need of the story. I can live life on life's own terms again, and I have even come to feel God's Spirit recalling me because God is not finished with my ministry. I feel I have come out of the darkness, back into God's wonderful Light. I want to affirm with deep thankfulness that God's power is far greater than the compulsive power of any addictive activity!